ROAD ATLAS

New England

CONTENTS

LEGEND

ROAD CLASSIFICATIONS

Interstate Highway
Controlled Access Highways
Toll Highways
Other Divided Highways
US Highways
State Highways
Connecting Roads

Airports
✈ Major
✈ Military
✈ Other
🎓 College, University
🗼 Lighthouse
Port of Entry

SPECIAL FEATURES

● Point of Interest
▲ State Forest
🎿 Ski Area
▲ Mountain
)(Notch
★ State Capitol
⌂ Covered Bridge

------- State Boundary
------- County Boundary
------- Community Boundary
------- Ferry Route
------- Trail
Park
Urban Area

HIGHWAY MARKERS

 Interstate   U.S.   State   ▪8 Interchange No.

The information in this publication has been obtained from various authoritative sources. Nevertheless, a work of this scope may contain some inaccuracies. While we have attempted to verify the information contained in this publication, no liability is assumed for damages, direct or consequential, arising from errors or omissions. Any errors or omissions called to our attention will be greatly appreciated. Please e-mail your comments to customerservice@americanmap.com and refer to the title of this publication.

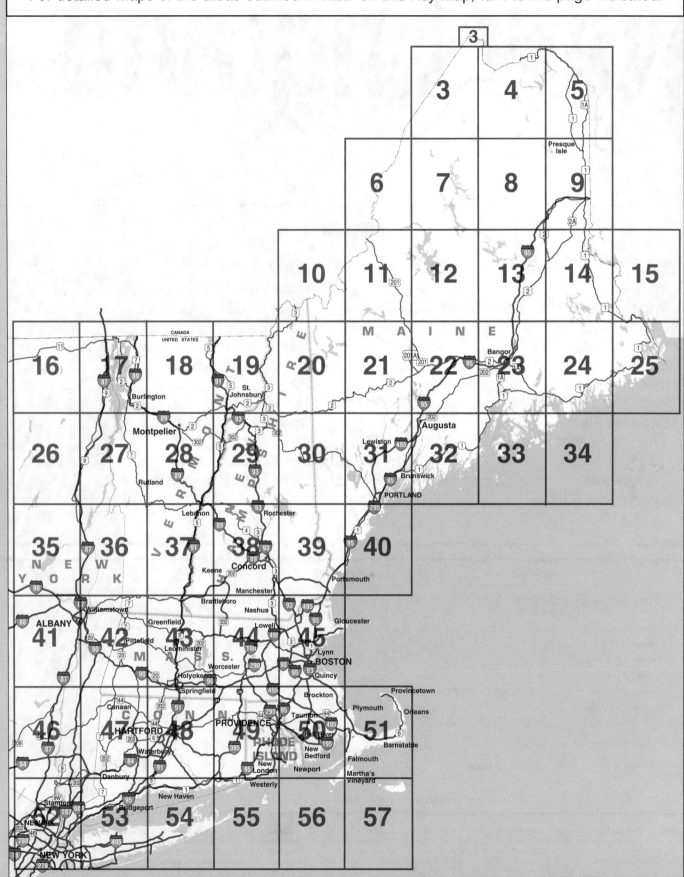

Quickly estimate distance:
Each grid box represents approximately
12.4 miles horizontally by 12.4 miles vertically.

Scale: 1:363,000
1 inch = 5.4 miles

0   .75   1.5 MILE
0   .75   1.5 KILOMETER

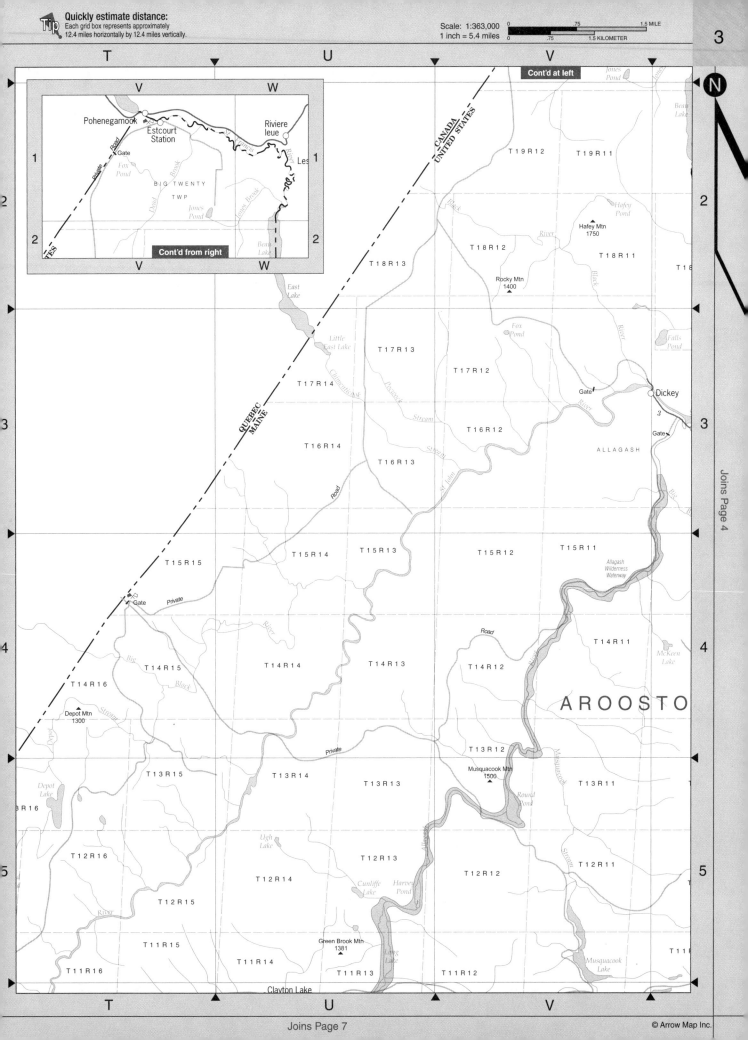

Cont'd at left

N

Pohenegamook

Estcourt Station

Riviere Ieue

Les

Gate

Fox Pond

BIG TWENTY TWP

Jones Pond

Jones Brook

Dead Brook

Beau Lake

Cont'd from right

Jones Pond

Beau Lake

CANADA
UNITED STATES

T 19 R 12   T 19 R 11

Black River

Hafey Pond

Hafey Mtn 1750

T 18 R 12   T 18 R 11   T 18

T 18 R 13

Rocky Mtn 1400

East Lake

Black River

Little East Lake

Fox Pond

Falls Pond

T 17 R 13   T 17 R 12

QUEBEC
MAINE

T 17 R 14

Chimenticook

Pescook Stream

Gate

River

Dickey

T 16 R 14   T 16 R 12

Stream

Gate

3

St. John Stream

ALLAGASH

T 16 R 13

Road

T 15 R 15   T 15 R 14   T 15 R 13   T 15 R 12   T 15 R 11

Allagash Wilderness Waterway

Gate   Private

River

Road

T 14 R 11

McKeen Lake

T 14 R 15   T 14 R 14   T 14 R 13   T 14 R 12

T 14 R 16

A R O O S T O

Depot Mtn 1300

Stream

Depot

Private

T 13 R 12

Musquacook

T 13 R 15   T 13 R 14   T 13 R 13

Musquacook Mtn 1500

T 13 R 11

Depot Lake

Round Pond

3 R 16

Ugh Lake

Allagash

Stream

T 12 R 16

T 12 R 13   T 12 R 12   T 12 R 11

T 12 R 14

Cunliffe Lake   Harvey Pond

T 12 R 15

River

Green Brook Mtn 1381

Long Lake

T 11 R 15

Musquacook Lake

T 11 R 16

T 11 R 14

T 11 R 13   T 11 R 12   T 11 R

Clayton Lake

Joins Page 4

N

2

Edmundston
Madawaska
MA

120

Caron
Brook
1 10
R St John
Upper
Frenchville
2
Frenchville

Fort Kent
Clair 7
Fort Kent
UMS
Fort Kent
FRENCHVILLE
162
St. Agatha

205 161
Wheelock
Bossy Mtn
1480
8
Lonesome Pines
Trails
FORT KENT
ST AGATHA

Connors
St John
Wheelock
Lake
7
9 161
Daigle
4

11
WALLAGRASS

St. Francis
ST FRANCIS
ST JOHN
PLT
R
Soldier
Pond
NEW CANADA
T17R5
Ouelette
4
162
Sincl

3

Dickey
161
Gate
Mc Lean Mtn
1954
Mc Lean
Lake
Wallagrass
Lake
Wallagrass
2
Plaisted
EAGLE LAKE
4
T16R9
T16R8
T16R6
T16R5
Square
Lake

Gate
Allagash
T15R9
R
Eagle Lake
Eagle Lake
T15R8
T15R6
T15R5

De Boulie Mtn
1981
Three Brooks Mtn
1578
5
Winterville
Quimby
WINTERVILLE
R

4

T14R10
T14R9
T14R8
T14R7
T14R6
T14R5

McKeen
Lake
Chase
Brook
17
Moose Mtn
1220

OSTOOK
Fish River
Lake
PORTAGE LAKE
T13R5

T13R10
T13R9
T13R8
T13R7
Portage
Gate

5

Carr Pond Mtn
1390
11
ASHLAND

T12R10
T12R9
T12R8
T12R7
Skerry
11
Frenchville

NASHVILLE PLT
Sheridan
227

T11R10
T11R8
Gate
Ashland
10

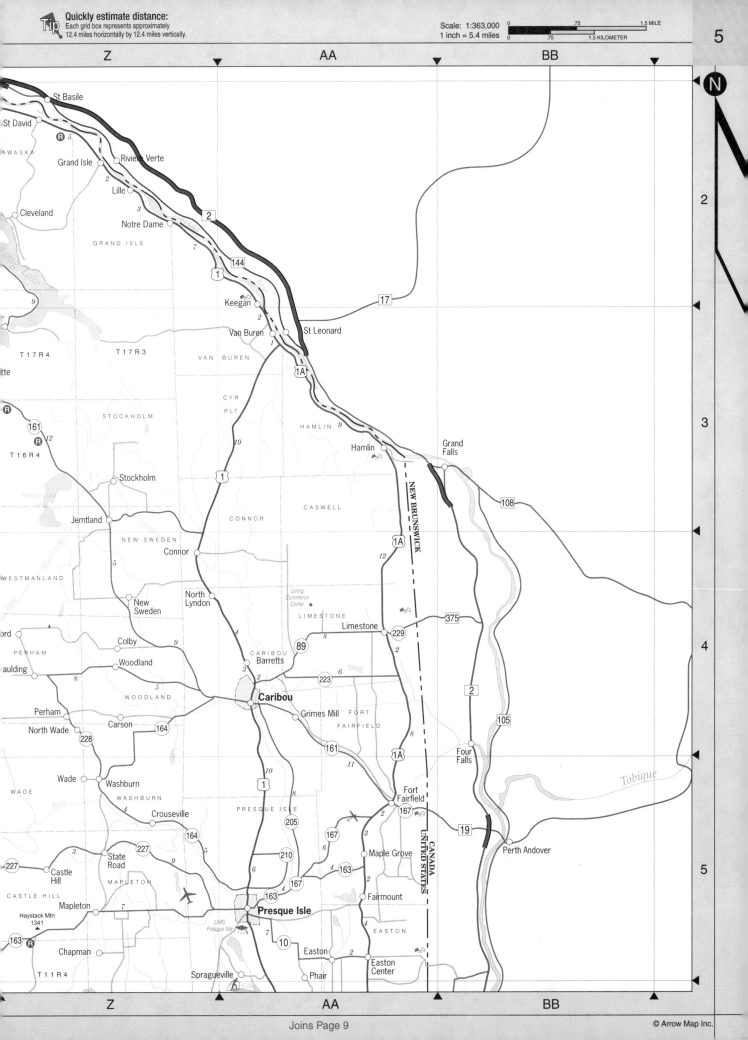

Tip Quickly estimate distance:
Each grid box represents approximately
12.4 miles horizontally by 12.4 miles vertically.

Scale: 1:363,000
1 inch = 5.4 miles

0   .75   1.5 MILE
0   .75   1.5 KILOMETER

5

Z   AA   BB

N

St Basile
St David
AWASKA
Grand Isle
Riviere Verte
Lille
Cleveland
Notre Dame
GRAND ISLE
2
144
1
Keegan
Van Buren
St Leonard
VAN BUREN
VAN BUREN
1A
CYR PLT
HAMLIN
Hamlin
Grand Falls
NEW BRUNSWICK
17
108
2

161
T 16 R 4
T 17 R 4
T 17 R 3
STOCKHOLM
Stockholm
1
Jemtland
NEW SWEDEN
Connor
CONNOR
CASWELL
1A
3

WESTMANLAND
New Sweden
North Lyndon
Loring Commerce Center
LIMESTONE
Limestone
229
375
4

ord
PERHAM
Colby
Woodland
89
CARIBOU
Barretts
223
2
105
aulding
WOODLAND
Caribou
Grimes Mill
FORT FAIRFIELD
Perth Andover
Tobique
Perham
North Wade
Carson
164
228
161
1A
Four Falls
19
WADE
Wade
Washburn
WASHBURN
1
Fort Fairfield
167
CANADA
UNITED STATES

Crouseville
PRESQUE ISLE
205
167
Maple Grove
227
164
210
167
163
State Road
MAPLETON
6
163
Fairmount
227
Castle Hill
CASTLE HILL
Mapleton
Haystack Mtn 1341
10
UMS Presque Isle
Presque Isle
EASTON
163
Chapman
T 11 R 4
Spragueville
Phair
Easton
Easton Center
5

N

Gate

Daaquam River

QUEBEC
MAINE

Gate

BIG TEN
T W P

SW Branch

St. Johns

T 9 R 18

T 9 R 17

Baker

Harwood Mtr
1300

St. Johns River

T 8 R 18

T 8 R 17

T 8 R 19

Southwest Branch

Branch

CANADA
UNITED STATES

T 7 R 19

Little

T 7 R 18

T 7 R 17

Baker
Lake

Gate

BIG SIX
TWP

T 6 R 18

T 6 R 17

Baker

Fifth
Pond

St Georges

T 5 R 19

T 5 R 18

T 5 R 17

Gate

T 5 R 20

Fourth
Pond

173

Nulhedus
1910

First
Pond

Third
Pond

Dole
Pond

Dole

Brook

COMSTOCK
TWP

Second
Pond

269

Frost
Pond

Dole
Pond

DOLE BROOK
TWP

North

Seboomook Mtn
2390

T 4 R 17

T 4 R 5

Long
Pond

Green Mtn
2395

Branch

Penobscot
Lake

Penobscot

St-Gedeon

HAMMOND
TWP

Pittston Farm

P L Y

PITTSTON ACADEMY

GRANT

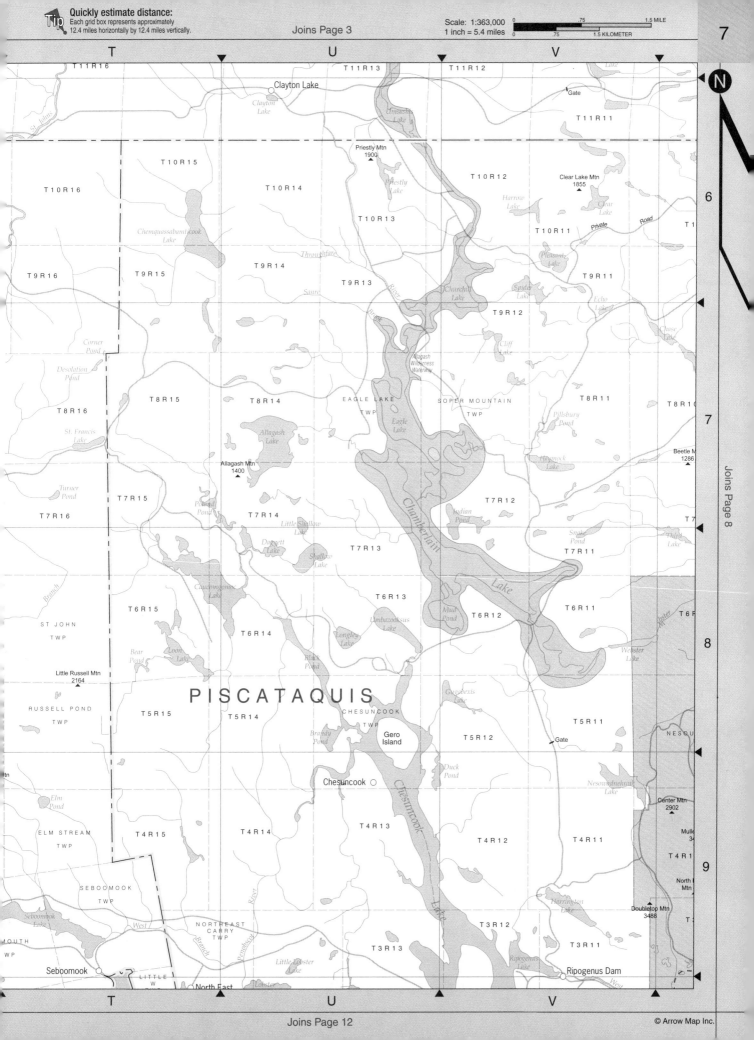

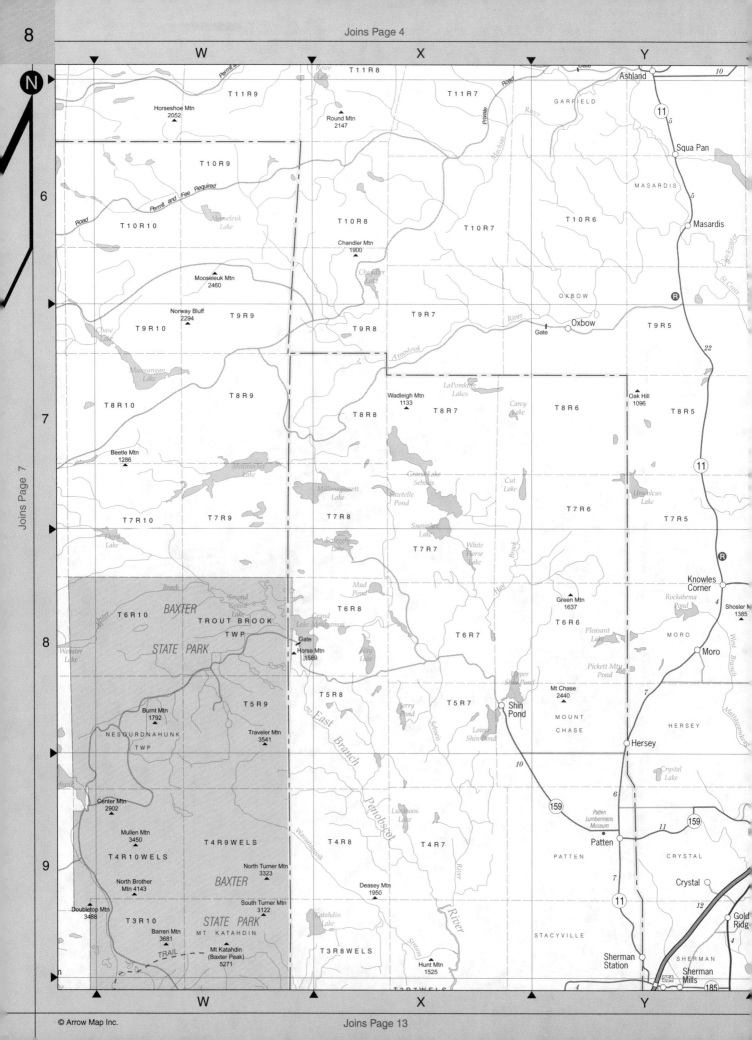

Quickly estimate distance:
Tip Each grid box represents approximately
12.4 miles horizontally by 12.4 miles vertically.

Scale: 1:363,000
1 inch = 5.4 miles

.75   1.5 MILE
0
.75   1.5 KILOMETER

Z   AA   BB

N

T 11 R 4   Spragueville   Phair   Center

CHAPMAN   14   1A

Echo Lake
Aroostook SP

Quoggy Joe Mtn
1213   WESTFIELD   Westfield   9   MARS

Squa Pan Mtn
1460   HILL

T 10 R 3   Big Rock   105   6

2

SQUAPAN TWP   Squa Pan Lake   Mars Hill

Blaine

River   E PLT   1   BLAINE   Florenceville

Robinson

T 9 R 3   COX   6   Centerville   110

PATENT

T 9 R 4   Saddleback Mtn
1695   Number 9 Mtn
1638   Bridgewater   560

Number 9 Lake   T D R 2   BRIDGE-
WATER   7

ST CROIX   T 8 R 3   8   Lakeville   104
TWP

TCR 2   MONTICELLO   Hartland

St. Croix Lake   Howe Brook Mtn
1110   Monticello

River   6

LITTLETON   103   105

WEBBERTOWN   DUDLEY   HAMMOND   Littleton   2

10

122   7

SMYRNA   LUDLOW   95   Woodstock

MERRILL   291   HOULTON   11   ?   302   2   95

Smyrna
Mills   6   Ludlow   2   10   305

5   New Limerick   Houlton   8

DYER   286   NEW LIMERICK
BROOK   Oakfield   Meduxnekeag Lake   Carys
Mills   540   7   4

OAKFIELD   Hodgdon

95   Dyer
Brook   7   Hodgdon
Corners

10   7   Pleasant Lake   LINNEUS   Linneus   HODGDON   2

R   Skitacook Lake   East Branch   15   Cary   4

Island
Falls   76   T 4 R 3   CARY PLT

ISLAND   Mattawamkeag Lake   TAR 2

FALLS   6   R   North
Amity   4

Caribou Lake   2A   AMITY   4

T 3 R 4   Mitchell Mtn
567   South
Amity   540

Macwahoc Lake   T 3 R 3   FORKSTOWN

CANADA
UNITED STATES

NEW BRUNSWICK
MAINE

St.

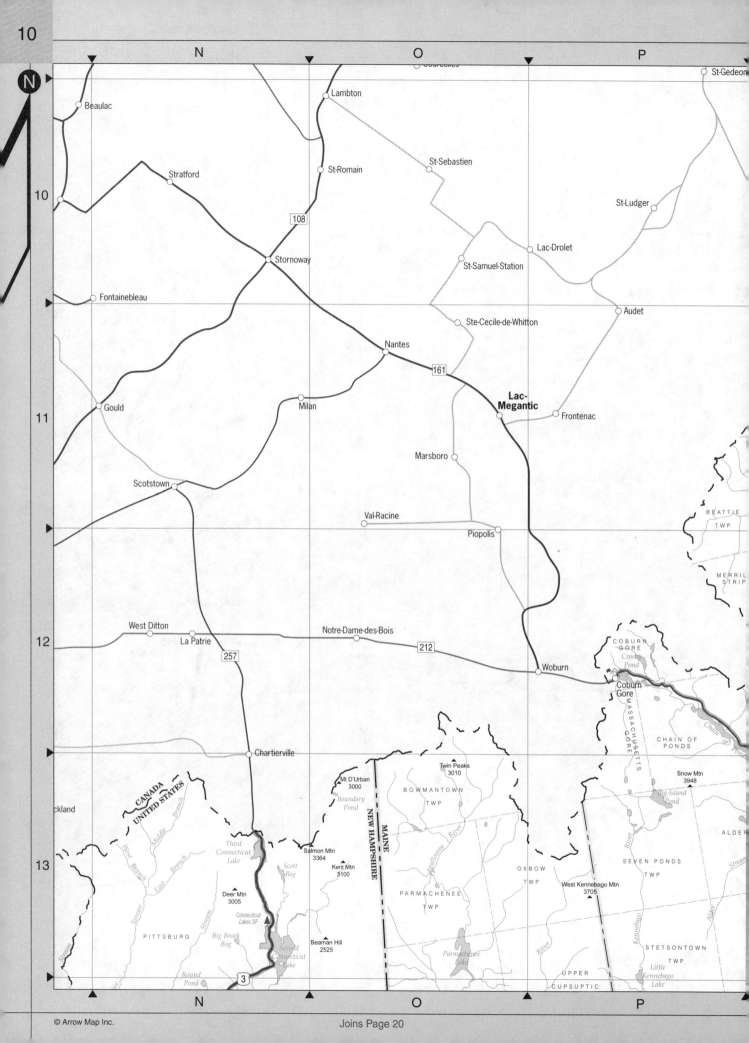

N

St-Gedeon

Beaulac

Lambton

Stratford

St-Romain

St-Sebastien

St-Ludger

10

108

Lac-Drolet

Stornoway

St-Samuel-Station

Fontainebleau

Audet

Ste-Cecile-de-Whitton

Nantes

161

Gould

Milan

Lac-Megantic

11

Frontenac

Marsboro

BEATTIE
TWP

Scotstown

Val-Racine

MERRIL
STRIP

Piopolis

West Ditton

Notre-Dame-des-Bois

COBURN
GORE
Crosby
Pond

12

La Patrie

212

257

Woburn

Coburn
Gore

CHAIN OF
PONDS

Snow Mtn
3948

Chartierville

Twin Peaks
3010

CANADA
UNITED STATES

Mt D'Urban
3000

BOWMANTOWN
TWP

Boundary
Pond

Big Island
Pond

ALDER

ckland

West Branch

Middle Branch

Third
Connecticut
Lake

Salmon Mtn
3364

MAINE
NEW HAMPSHIRE

Swattoway River

OXBOW
TWP

West Kennebago Mtn
3705

SEVEN PONDS
TWP

Scott
Bog

Kent Mtn
3100

13

East Branch

Deer Mtn
3005

Connecticut
Lakes SF

PARMACHENEE
TWP

Kennebago River

River

Alder Stream

Stream

PITTSBURG

Big Brook
Bog

Beaman Hill
2525

STETSONTOWN
TWP

Second
Connecticut
Lake

Parmachenee
Lake

Round
Pond

3

UPPER
CUPSUPTIC

Little
Kennebago
Lake

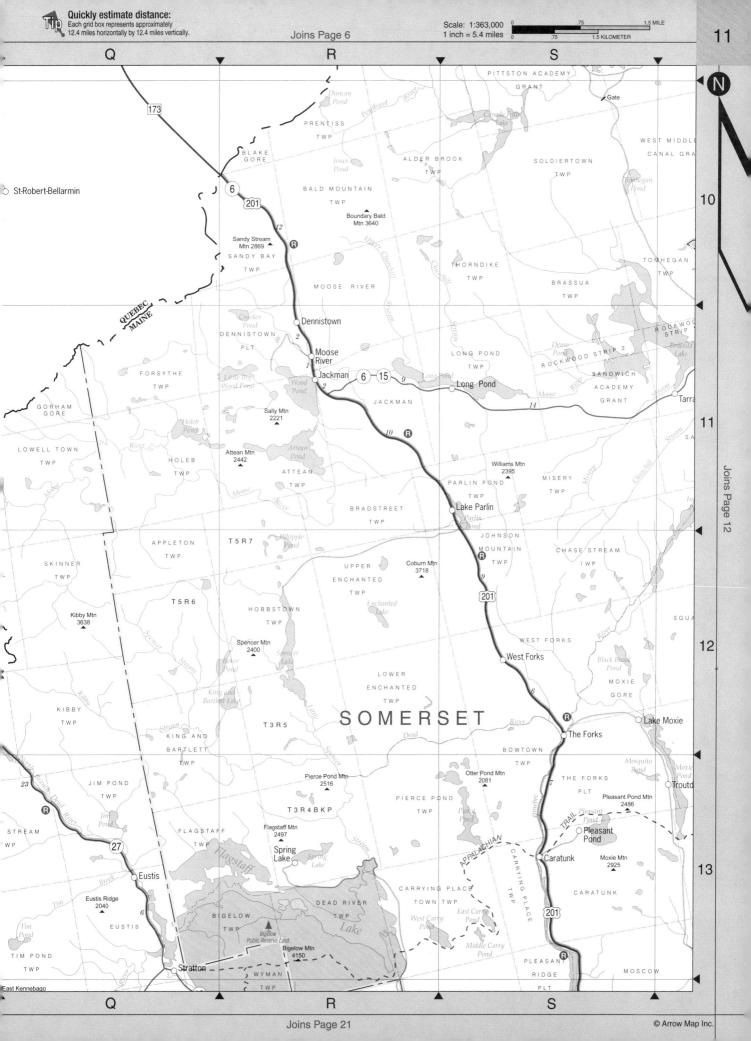

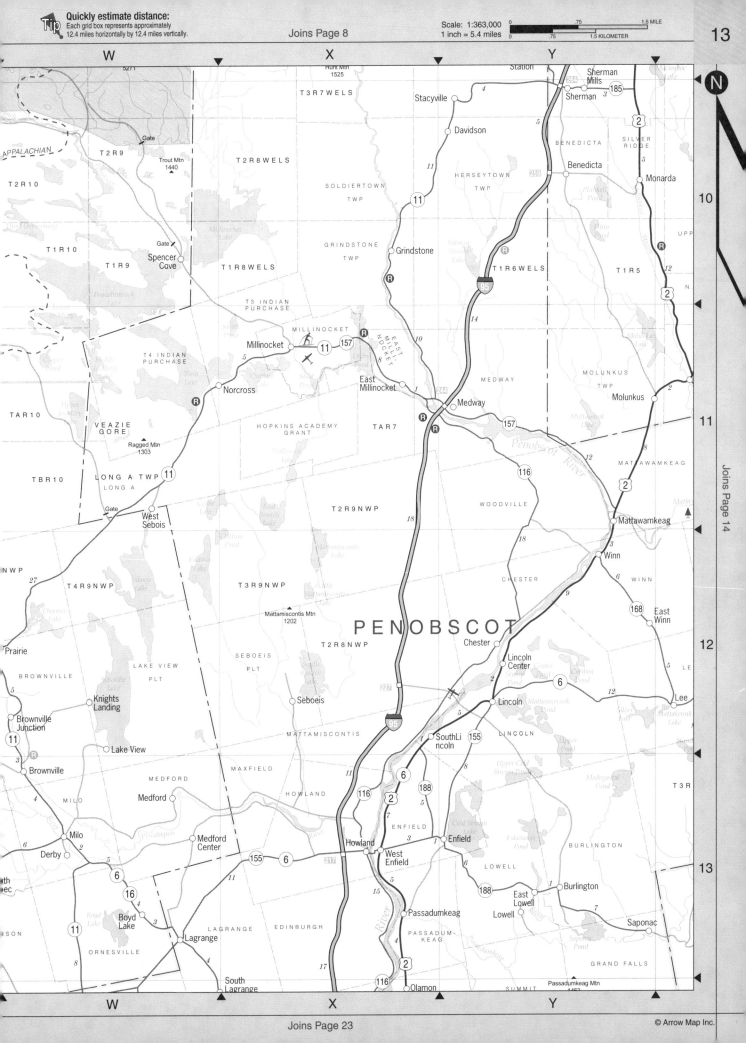

© Arrow Map Inc.

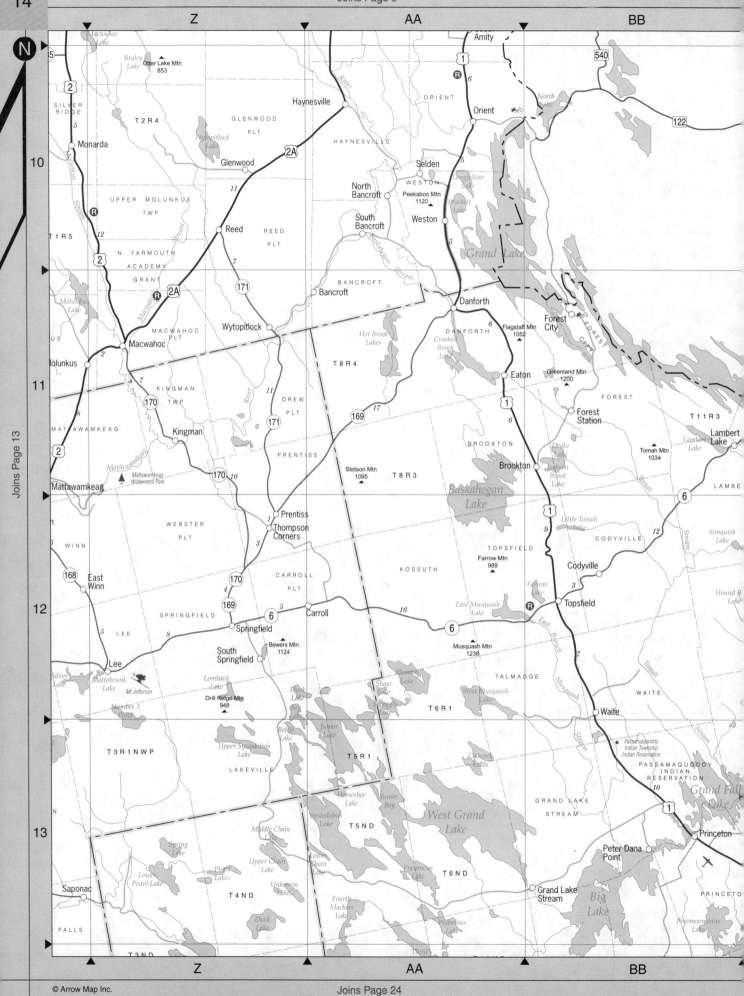

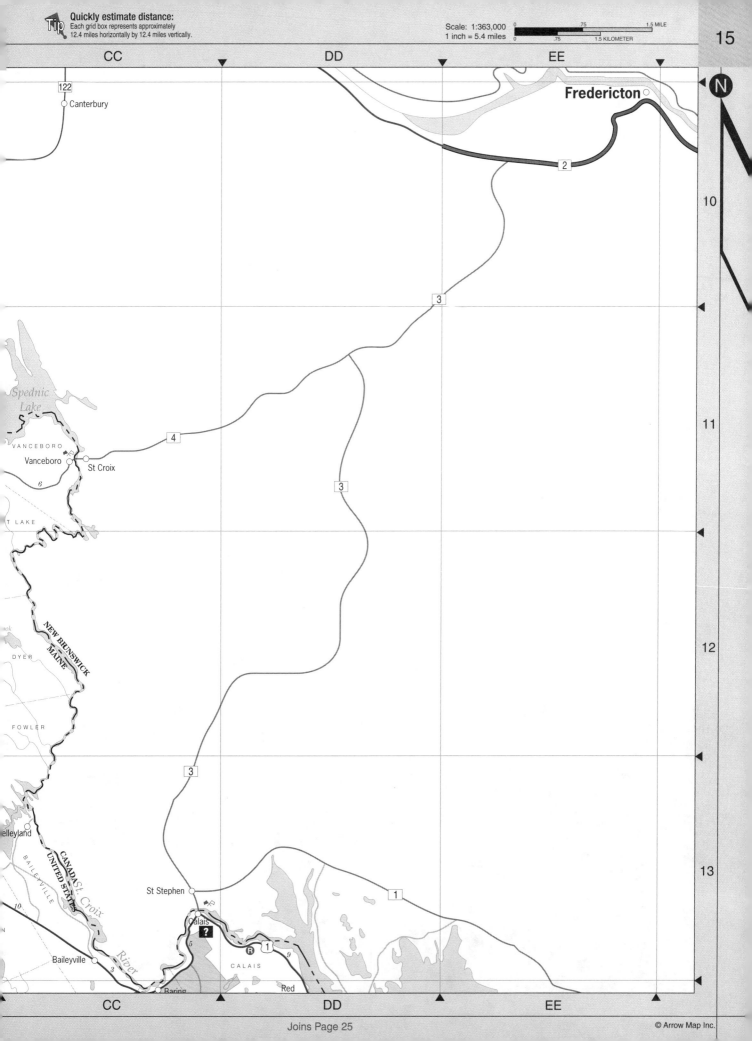

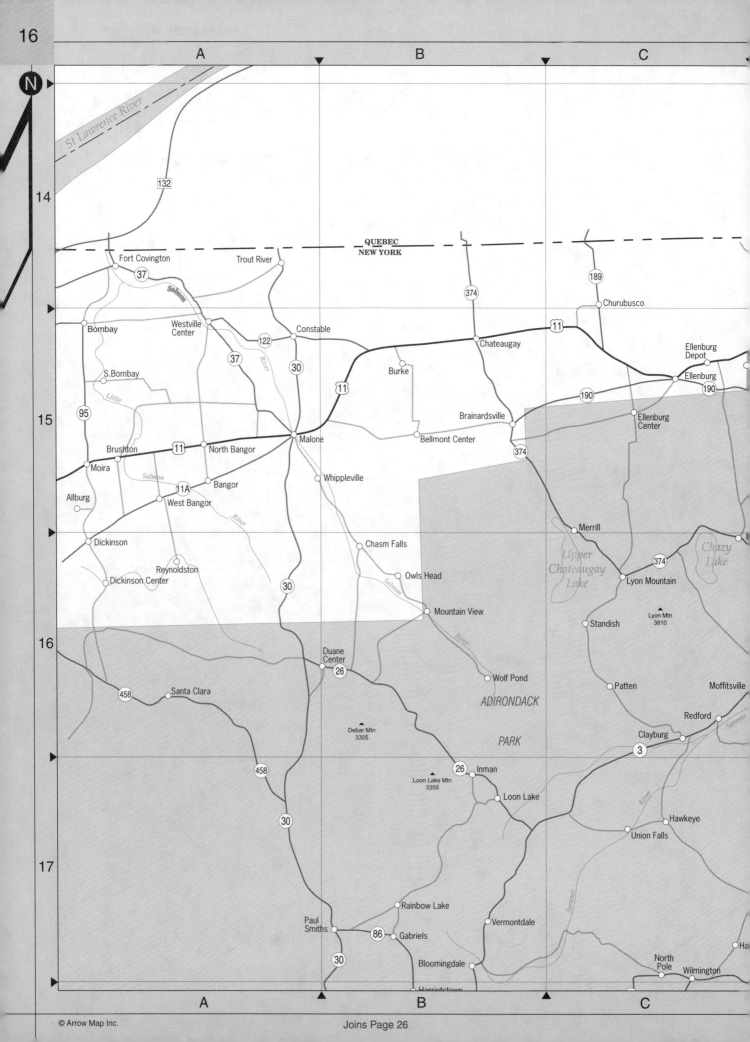

Joins Page 26

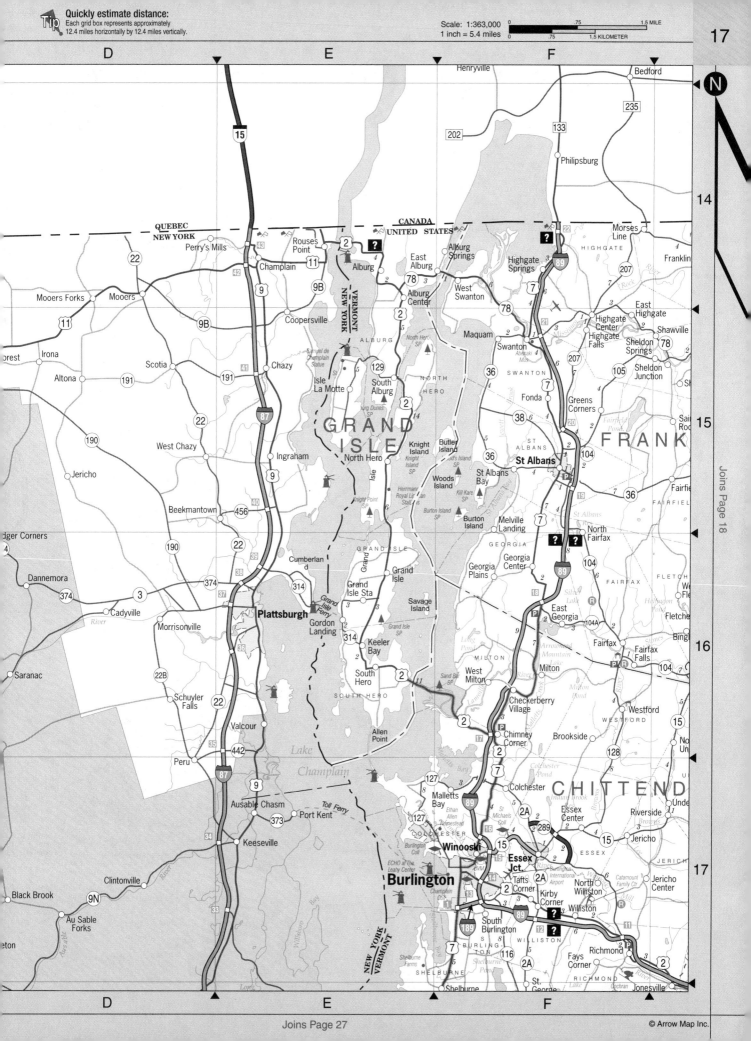

Quickly estimate distance:
Each grid box represents approximately
12.4 miles horizontally by 12.4 miles vertically.

Scale: 1:363,000
1 inch = 5.4 miles

1.5 MILE

1.5 KILOMETER

N

Joins Page 18

15

16

17

Bedford

235

Henryville

202

133

Philipsburg

CANADA
UNITED STATES

QUEBEC
NEW YORK

Perry's Mills

43

Rouses
Point

2

Alburg
Springs

Morses
Line

22

Franklin

HIGHGATE

Highgate
Springs

89

207

East
Highgate

15

22

Champlain

11

9

Alburg

East
Alburg

78

West
Swanton

78

Maquam

7

Swanton

207

Highgate
Center

Highgate
Falls

Shawville

78

Sheldon
Springs

Mooers Forks

Mooers

9B

Coopersville

9B

2

Alburg
Center

2

North Hero
SP

36

21

Sheldon
Junction

105

11

VERMONT
NEW YORK

ALBURG

NORTH
HERO

36

Fonda

20

7

Greens
Corners

Sai
Ro

Forest

Irona

Scotia

Chazy

41

191

129

South
Alburg

Isle
La Motte

2

38

104

St
ALBANS

FRANK

Fairfie

Altona

191

22

87

GRAND

ISLE

Knight
Island

Knight
Island
SP

Butler
Island

St Albans

36

St Albans
Bay

St Albans

SWANTON

Fairfield
Pond

FAIRFIEL

FAIRFIELD

West Chazy

22

190

Jericho

North Hero

Isle

Woods
Island

Woods
Island
SP

Herrman
Royal Li an
Stall ris

Kill Kare
SP

Melville
Landing

7

North
Fairfax

104

Fairfie

36

Beekmantown

456

9

GRAND ISLE

Burton Island
SP

Burton
Island

Georgia

Georgia
Center

FAIRFAX

FLETCH

W
Fle

dger Corners

190

22

39

Cumberlan
d

314

Grand
Isle Sta

Grand
Isle

Savage
Island

Georgia
Plains

89

104

Fletche

Dannemora

374

3

38

Grand
Isle
Ferry

314

Grand Isle
SP

18

East
Georgia

104A

Fairfax

Bing

374

Cadyville

37

Gordon
Landing

Keeler
Bay

MILTON

Arrowhead
Mountain
Lake

Fairfax
Falls

104

River

36

South
Hero

2

West
Milton

11

Milton

Long
Pond

Milton
Pond

Westford

15

Saranac

22B

Sand Bar
SP

WESTFORD

Schuyler
Falls

22

Valcour

9

Allen
Point

SOUTH HERO

Checkerberry
Village

2

Chimney
Corner

Brookside

128

No
Un

442

Lake

17

7

Colchester
Pond

CHITTEND

Peru

35

Champlain

2

Colchester

Westford

15

Jericho

Ausable Chasm

34

442

Toll Ferry

Port Kent

373

127

Malletts
Bay

127

Ethan
Allen
Homestead

89

16

St
Michaels
Coll

2A

289

15

Essex
Center

Riverside

Und

JERICH

Essex

Keeseville

ECHO at The
Leahy Center

Winooski

Burlington
Coll

15

Essex
Jct.

2A

Burlington
International
Airport

North
Williston

Jericho
Center

Catamount
Family Ctr

Clintonville

Burlington

13

14

2

Tafts
Corner

Kirby
Corner

89

Williston

11

9N

Black Brook

33

189

South
Burlington

116

12

Richmond

2

Au Sable
Forks

7

BURLING-
TON

2A

Fays
Corner

RICHMOND

Jonesville

ton

NEW YORK
VERMONT

Shelburne
Farms

Shelburne
Pond

St.
George

SHELBURNE

Shelburne

RICHMOND

River

N

14

15

16

17

Joins Page 17

QUEBEC
VERMONT

Bedford   Dunham   Sutton   Mansonville

Lac Memphremagog

Frelighsburg   Abercorn   Highwater

Morses Line   Franklin   East Franklin   West Berkshire   Richford   East Richford   North Troy

Franklin   Berkshire   Stevens Mill   Jay   Newport Center   Newport

Lake Carmi   RICHFORD   JAY   North Jay Pk 3400   Big Falls

East Highgate   Shawville   South Franklin   North Enosburg   East Berkshire   South Richford   Jay Pk 3861   Jay Peak SF   Westfield   Troy   Coventry

Sheldon Springs   North Sheldon   Enosburg Falls   Montgomery   Gilpin Mtn 2940   Buchanan Mtn 2940

Sheldon Junction   Sheldon   East Sheldon   Enosburg Center   Montgomery Center   WESTFIELD

FRANKLIN   ORLEANS

Saint Rocks   West Enosburg   Bordoville   East Enosburg   Hazen's Notch   Hazens Notch 1790   IRASBURG   Coventry

Fairfield Station   President Chester Arthur Birthplace   BAKERSFIELD   MONTGOMERY   Haystack Mtn 3223   LOWELL   Irasburg

Fairfield   East Fairfield   Bakersfield   BELVIDERE   Belvidere Mtn 3360   Lowell

Gilson Mtn 1900   Metcalf Pond   Belvidere Center   Belvidere Corners   Long Pond   Mt Norris 2575   ALBANY   West Glover

FLETCHER   Belvidere Junction   EDEN   Eden Mills   Albany   East Albany   Glover

West Fletcher   East Fletcher   Laraway Mtn 2780   Eden   Lake Eden   South Albany   GLOVER

Fletcher   Waterville   Butternut Mtn 2715   North Hyde Park   CRAFTSBURY   Mill Village   Craftsbury Common

Fairfax Falls   Binghamville   North Cambridge   JOHNSON   South Pond   HYDE PARK   East Craftsbury

Cambridge   Cambridge Junction   Johnson State College   Centerville   Craftsbury   GREENSBORO

Jeffersonville   Sterling Ridge   Johnson   East Johnson   HYDE PARK   North Wolcott   Long Pond

Westford   CAMBRIDGE   South Cambridge   LAMOILLE   Hyde Park   Garfield   WOLCOTT   Lake Eligo   Greensboro

North Underhill   Pleasant Valley   Smugglers Notch SP   Sterling Mtn 3715   Cady's Falls   Caspian Lake   Greensboro Bend

CHITTENDEN   Smugglers Notch 2162   Madonna Peak 3640   MORRISTOWN   Morrisville   Lake Elmore   Wolcott   HARDWICK   Hardwick Center   Stannard

Underhill Flats   Mt Mansfield 4393   Spruce Peak 3320   Morristown   Elmore SP   Hardwick   East Hardwick

Riverside   Underhill Center   The Pinnacle 2180   Elmore Mtn 2608   Mackville   North Walden

Jericho   Mt Clark 2960   Moss Glen Falls   ELMORE   CALEDONIA   Mackville

Jericho Center   Mt Mayo 3143   Lake Mansfield   Stowe   Mackville   South Walden   Walden Station   Walden

Catamount Family Ctr   Bolton Mtn 3680   Trapp Family Lodge   Stowe Lower Village   Mt Worcester 3286   Woodbury   Buck Lake

West Bolton   Bolton Valley Ski Area   Mt Mansfield SF   Moscow   WORCESTER   South Woodbury   WOODBURY   CABOT

Black Bear Inn   Ricker Mtn 3401   Waterbury Reservoir   White Rock Mtn 3194   Mt Hunger 3539   North Calais   Cabot   Cabot Creamery

Jonesville   BOLTON   WATERBURY   Waterbury   Maple   South Woodbury   Lower Cabot   Mollys Pond

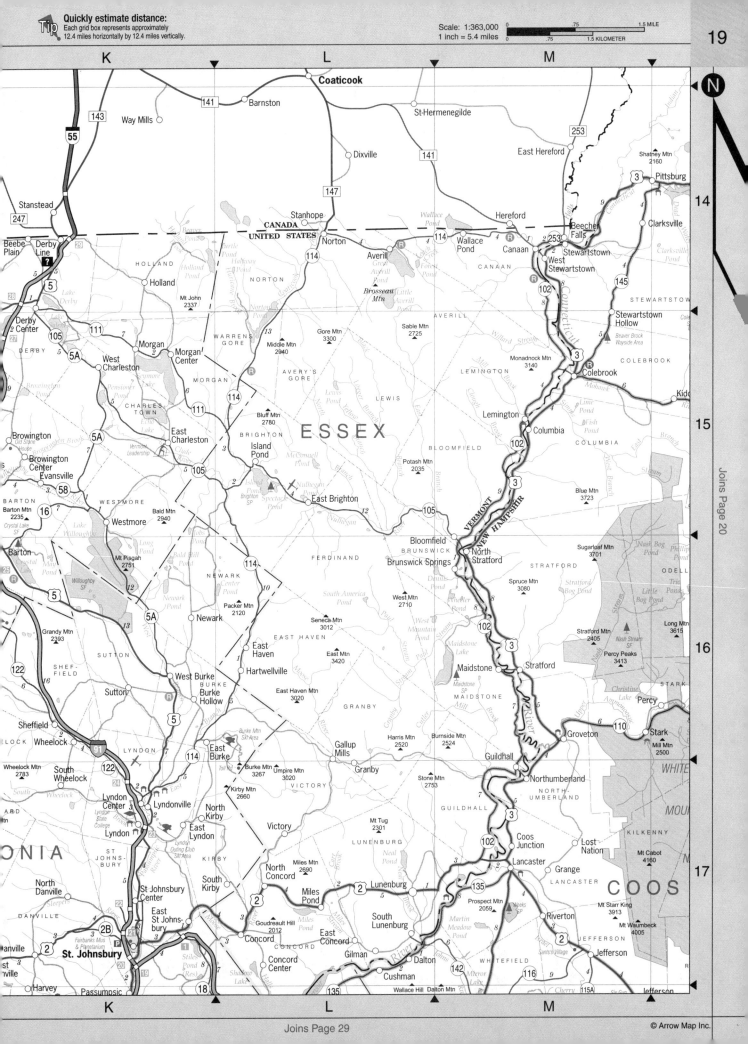

Quickly estimate distance:
Each grid box represents approximately
12.4 miles horizontally by 12.4 miles vertically.

Scale: 1:363,000
1 inch = 5.4 miles

0   .75   1.5 MILE
0   .75   1.5 KILOMETER

N

14

15

16

17

Joins Page 20

© Arrow Map Inc.

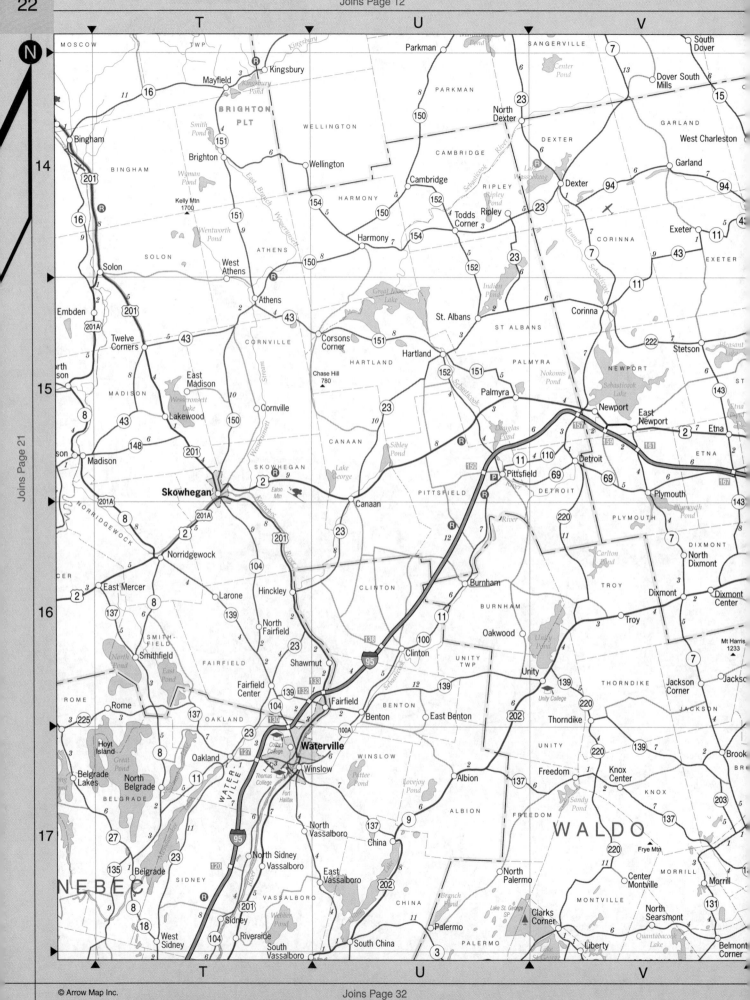

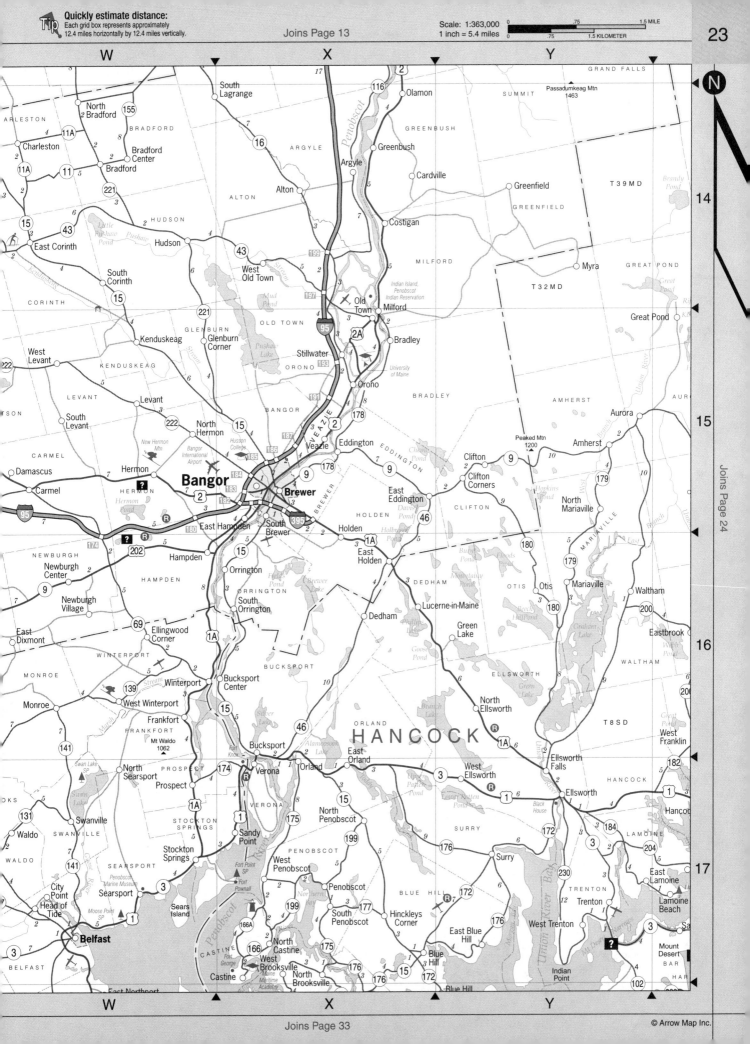

Quickly estimate distance:
Each grid box represents approximately
12.4 miles horizontally by 12.4 miles vertically.

Joins Page 13

Scale: 1:363,000
1 inch = 5.4 miles

23

0   .75   1.5 MILE
0   .75   1.5 KILOMETER

W   X   Y

N

14

Joins Page 24

15

16

17

W   X   Y

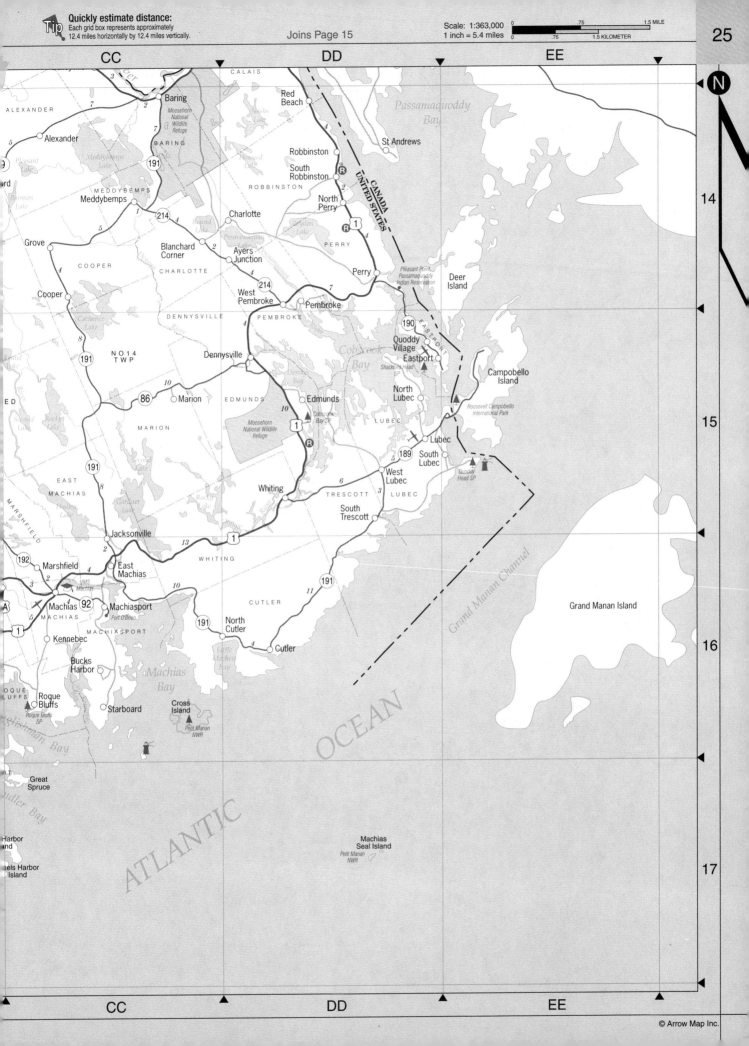

Quickly estimate distance:
Each grid box represents approximately
12.4 miles horizontally by 12.4 miles vertically.

Scale: 1:363,000
1 inch = 5.4 miles

.75   1.5 MILE
.75   1.5 KILOMETER

N

CC   DD   EE

14

CALAIS
Red
Beach

Baring

ALEXANDER   Moosehorn
                             National
                             Wildlife
                             Refuge

Alexander   B A R I N G

Passamaquoddy
Bay

St Andrews

Robbinston

South
Robbinston

191

Meddybemps

R O B B I N S T O N

North
Perry

Charlotte   1

214

Blanchard
Corner

Ayers
Junction

P E R R Y

Perry

Pleasant Point
Passamaquoddy
Indian Reservation

Deer
Island

Grove

C O O P E R

214

West
Pembroke

Cooper   Catharce
                Lake

D E N N Y S V I L L E

Pembroke

P E M B R O K E

Cobscook
Bay

190

E A S T P O R T

Quoddy
Village

Eastport

Campobello
Island

Dennysville

Shackford Head
SP

191

N O 14
T W P

Denny's
Bay

North
Lubec

Roosevelt Campobello
International Park

86

Marion

E D M U N D S

Edmunds

Cobscook
Bay SP

L U B E C

1

Moosehorn
National Wildlife
Refuge

M A R I O N

Lubec

191

189

South
Lubec

Quoddy
Head SP

West
Lubec

E A S T
M A C H I A S

Whiting

T R E S C O T T

L U B E C

South
Trescott

Jacksonville   13

1

M A R S H F I E L D

192   Marshfield

W H I T I N G

East
Machias

191

Grand Manan Island

92   Machiasport

M A C H I A S

Machias

C U T L E R

Kennebec

M A C H I A S P O R T

191

North
Cutler

Bucks
Harbor

Cutler

ROQUE
BLUFFS

Roque
Bluffs

Roque Bluffs
SP

Starboard

Cross
Island

Petit Manan
NWR

Machias
Bay

ATLANTIC   OCEAN

Great
Spruce

Grand Manan Channel

Machias
Seal Island

Petit Manan
NWR

15

16

17

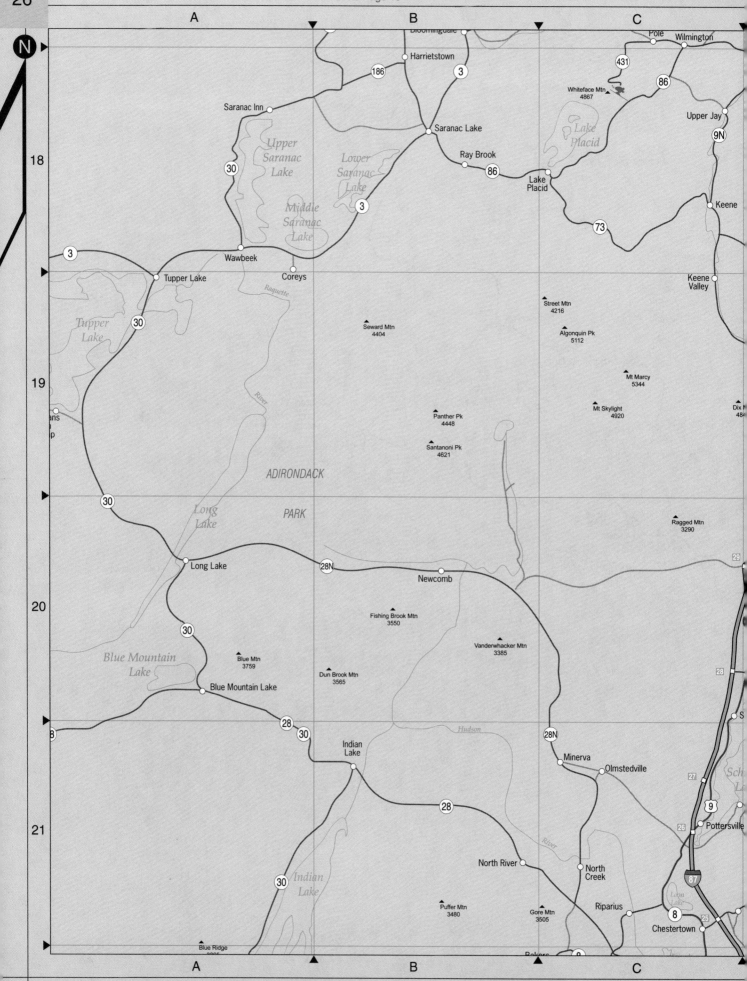

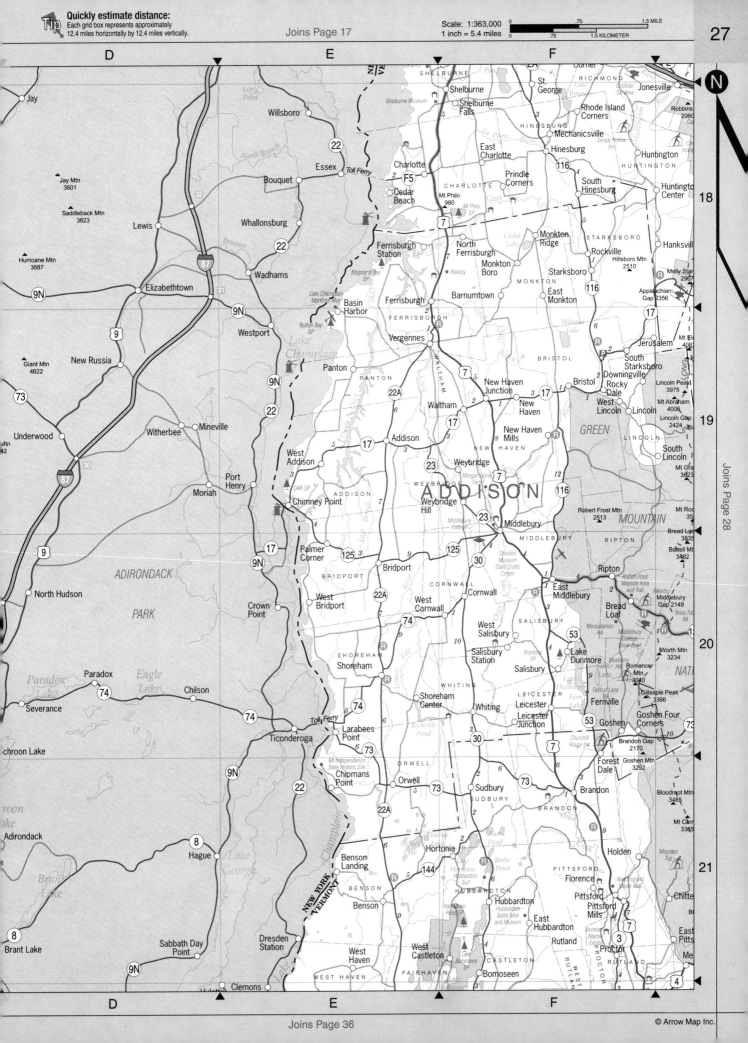

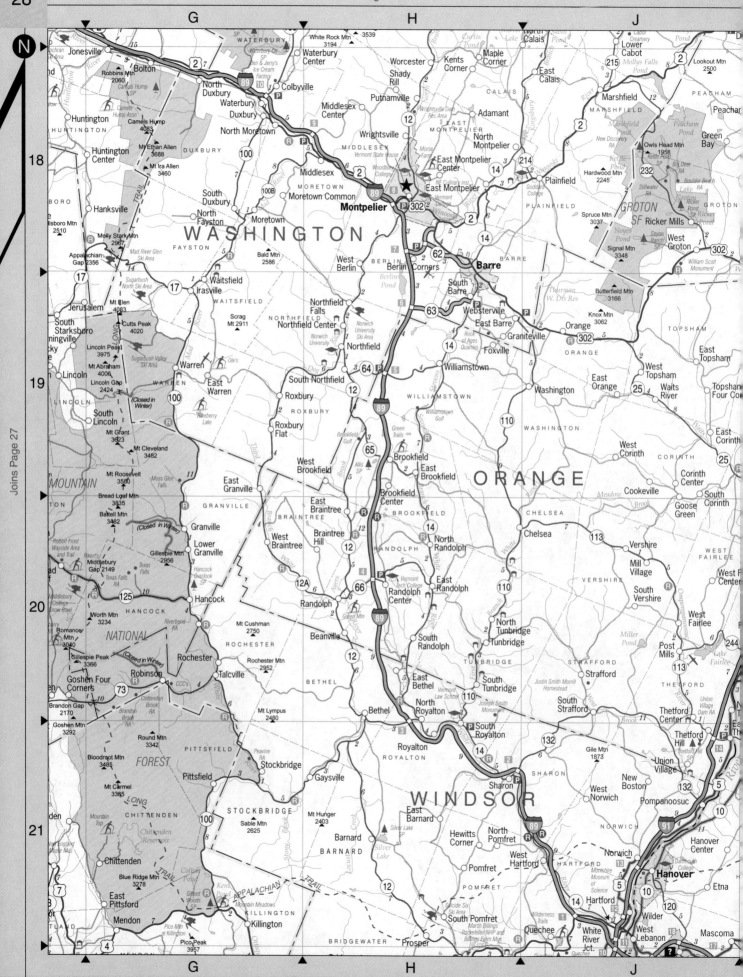

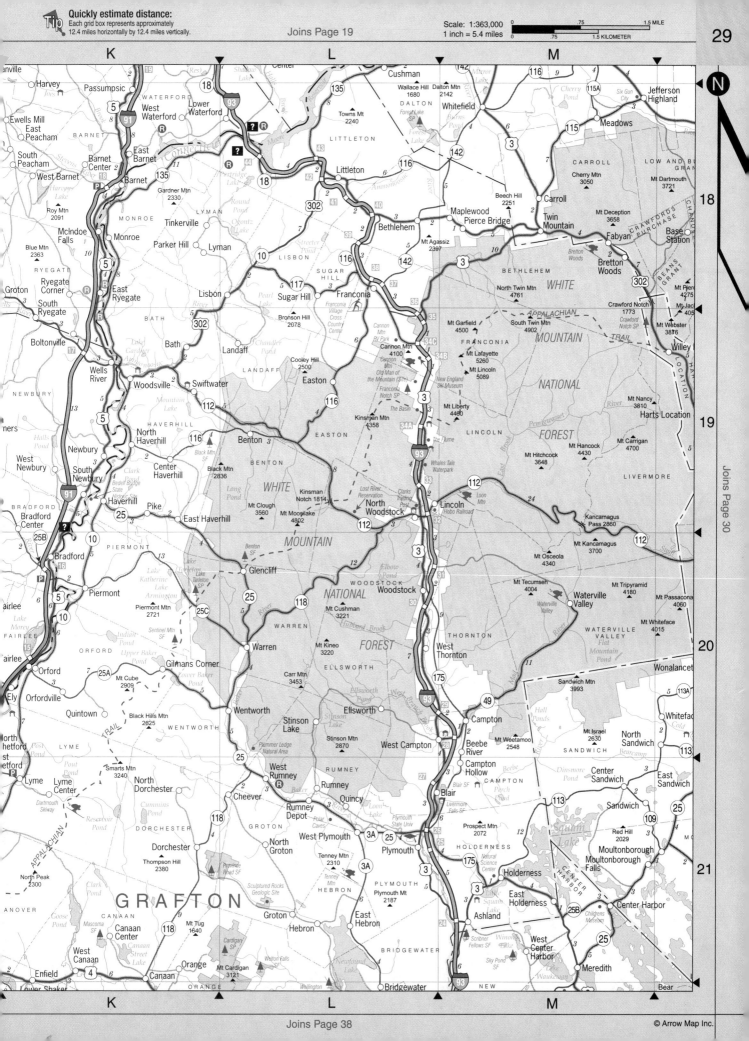

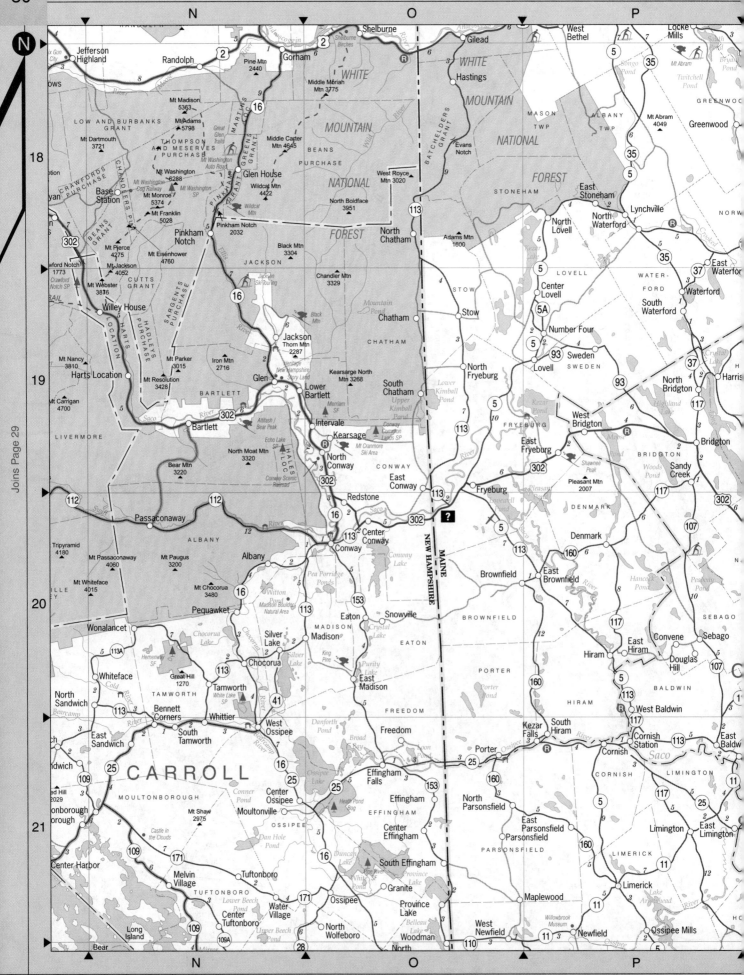

Joins Page 29

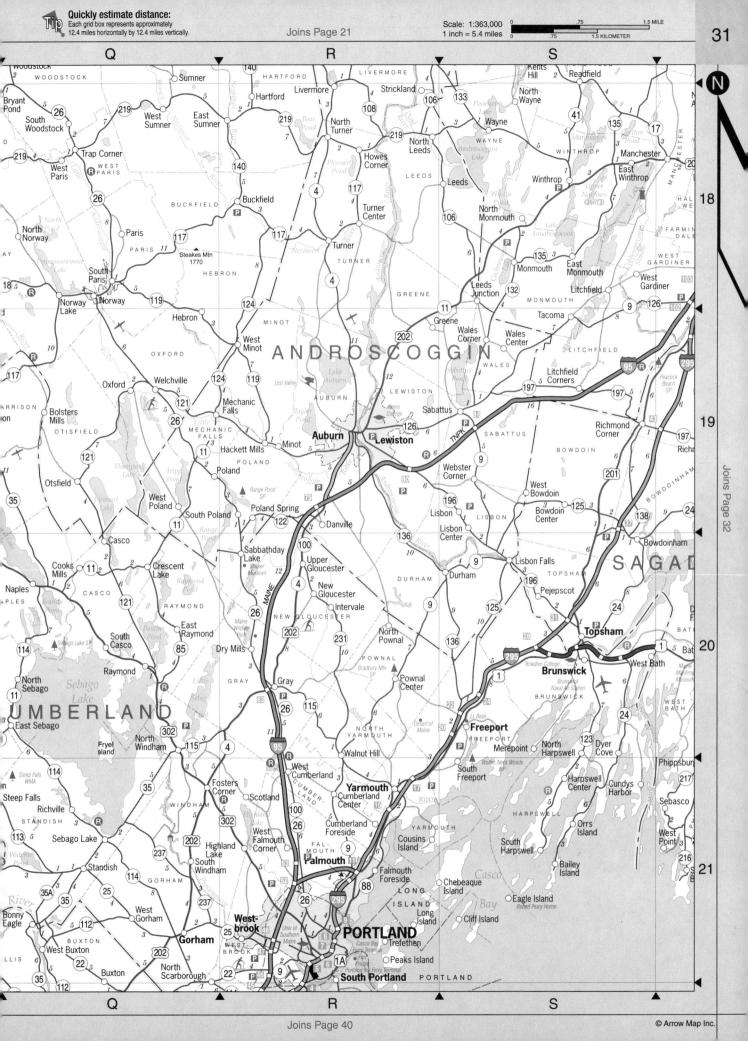

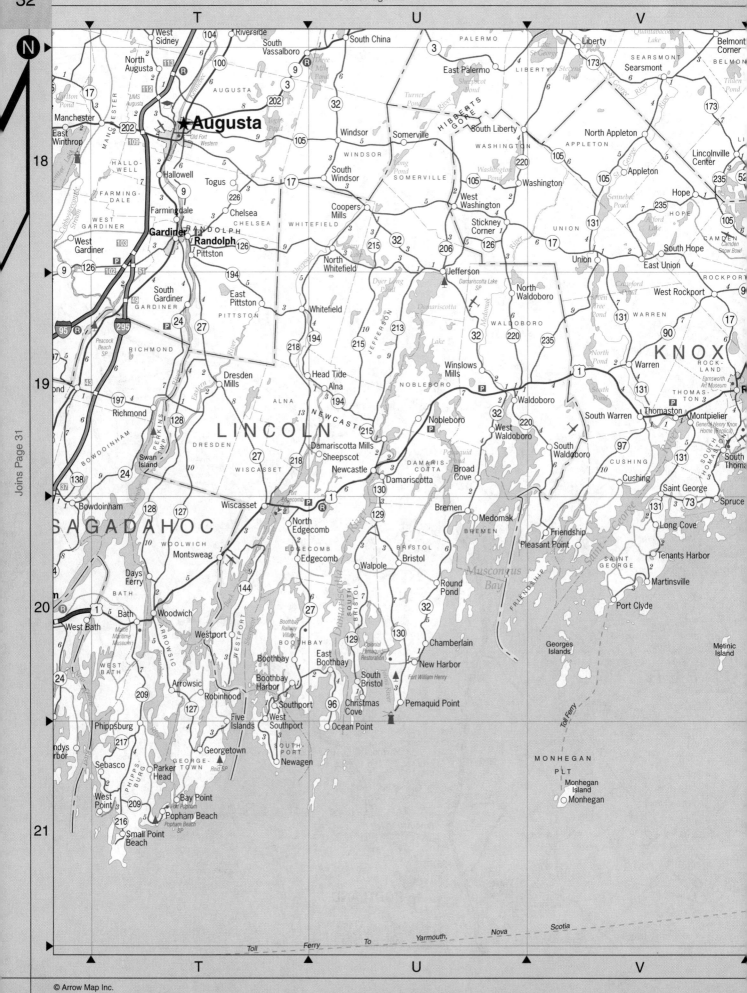

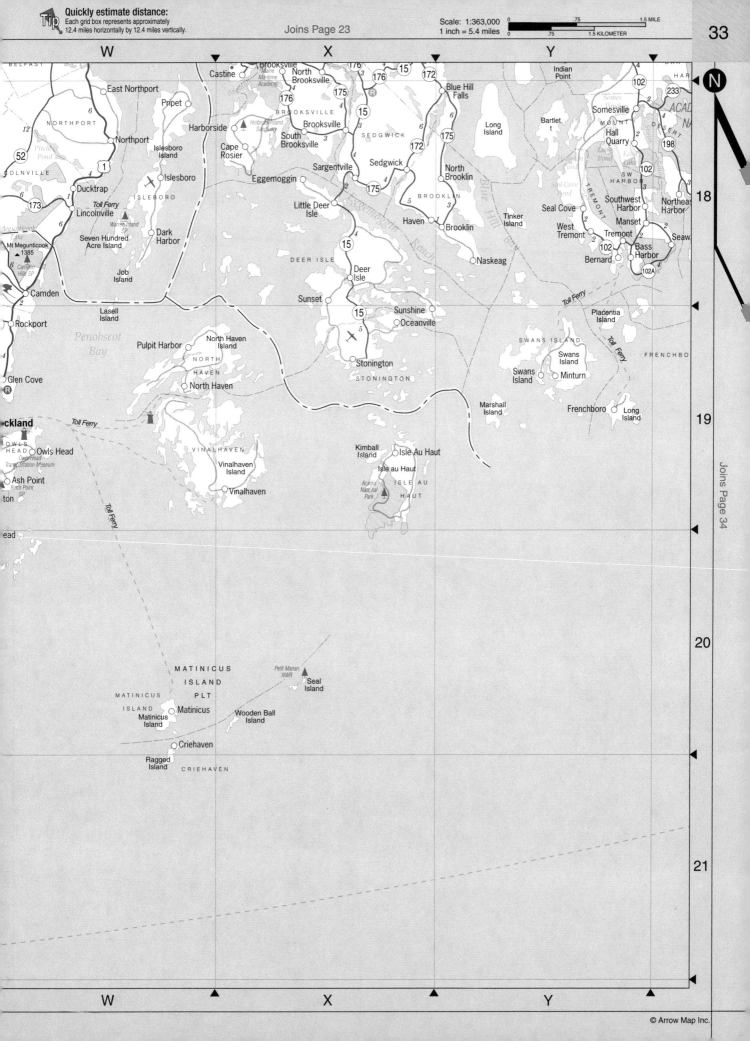

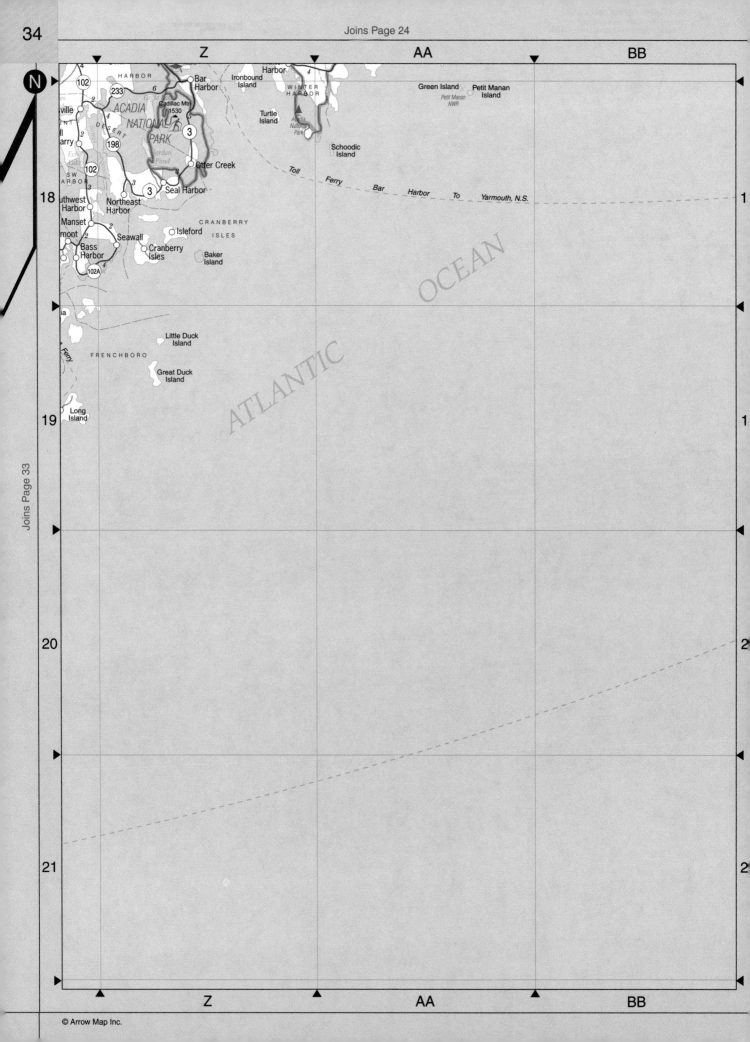

N

Joins Page 33

HARBOR

102
233

ACADIA NATIONAL PARK

Cadillac Mtn
1530

DESERT

Jordan Pond

198

102

SW HARBOR

3

3

Bar Harbor

Ironbound Island

WINTER HARBOR

Turtle Island

Acadia National Park

Green Island

Petit Manan Island

Petit Manan NWR

Schoodic Island

Otter Creek

Seal Harbor

18

1

Southwest Harbor

Northeast Harbor

Manset

mont

Bass Harbor

Seawall

Isleford

CRANBERRY ISLES

Cranberry Isles

Baker Island

102A

Toll Ferry Bar Harbor To Yarmouth, N.S.

OCEAN

ia

Little Duck Island

FRENCHBORO

Great Duck Island

Ferry

ATLANTIC

19

1

Long Island

20

2

21

2

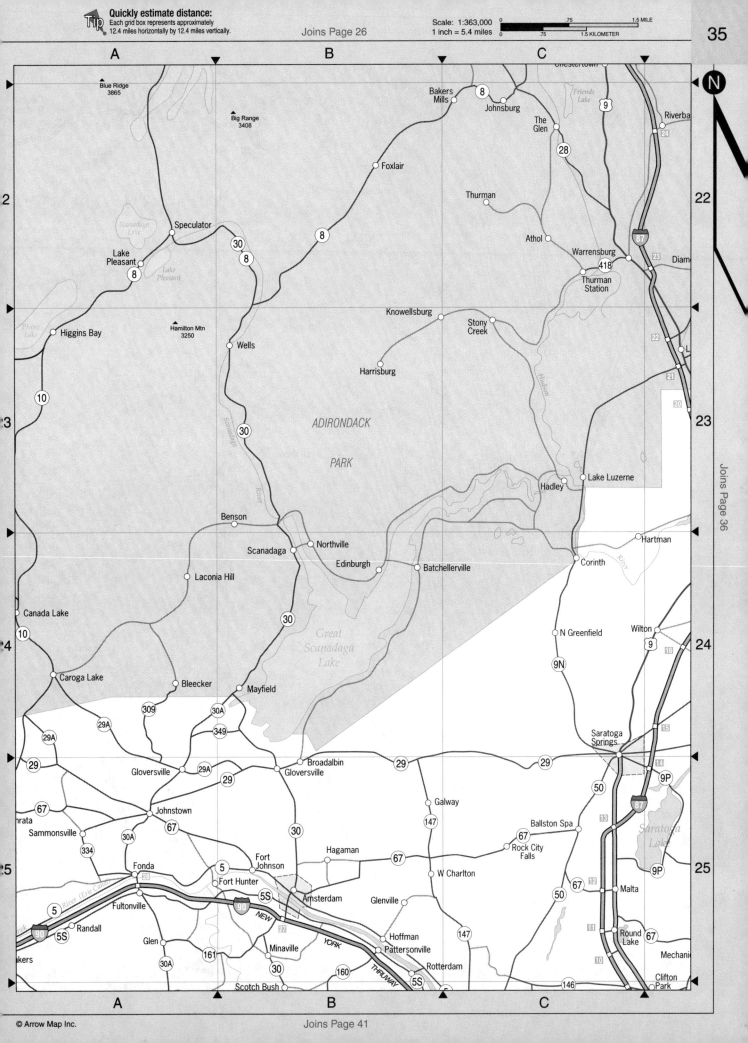

Quickly estimate distance:
Each grid box represents approximately
12.4 miles horizontally by 12.4 miles vertically.

Scale: 1:363,000
1 inch = 5.4 miles

0   .75   1.5 MILE
0   .75   1.5 KILOMETER

N

A   B   C

Blue Ridge
3865

Big Range
3408

Bakers
Mills   8
        Johnsburg

Chestertown

Friends
Lake   9

Riverba

24

Foxlair

The
Glen

28

Thurman

22

Scanadaga
Lake   Speculator

30

8

Athol

Warrensburg

87

Lake
Pleasant
        8   8

Lake
Pleasant

Thurman
Station   418

23

Diam

Piseco
Lake

Higgins Bay

Hamilton Mtn
3250   Wells

Knowellsburg

Stony
Creek

22

Hudson

21

10

Harrisburg

20

30

ADIRONDACK

PARK

Hadley

Lake Luzerne

23

Benson

Scanadaga

Scanadaga
River

Northville

Laconia Hill

Edinburgh

Batchellerville

Corinth

Hartman

River

Canada Lake

30

Great
Scanadaga
Lake

N Greenfield

Wilton

10

9N

9

16

24

Caroga Lake

Bleecker

Mayfield

Saratoga
Springs

15

309

30A

29A

349

29A

Broadalbin

29

29

14

9P

29

Gloversville

29A

Gloversville

50

9P

29

67

Galway

Ballston Spa

13

Saratoga
Lake

Johnstown

67

147

67

Rock City
Falls

50

rata

Sammonsville

30A

Hagaman

67

W Charlton

67

12

Fonda

334

5

30

Malta

28

Fort
Johnson

67

11

10

87

Round
Lake   67

Fulton ville

5

Fort Hunter

5S

Amsterdam

Glenville

9P

Mechani

5

Randall

5S

Glen

Minaville

161

27

NEW

YORK

Hoffman

Pattersonville

147

Clifton
Park

30A

30

160

Rotterdam

5S

146

Scotch Bush

A   B   C

N

Joins Page 36

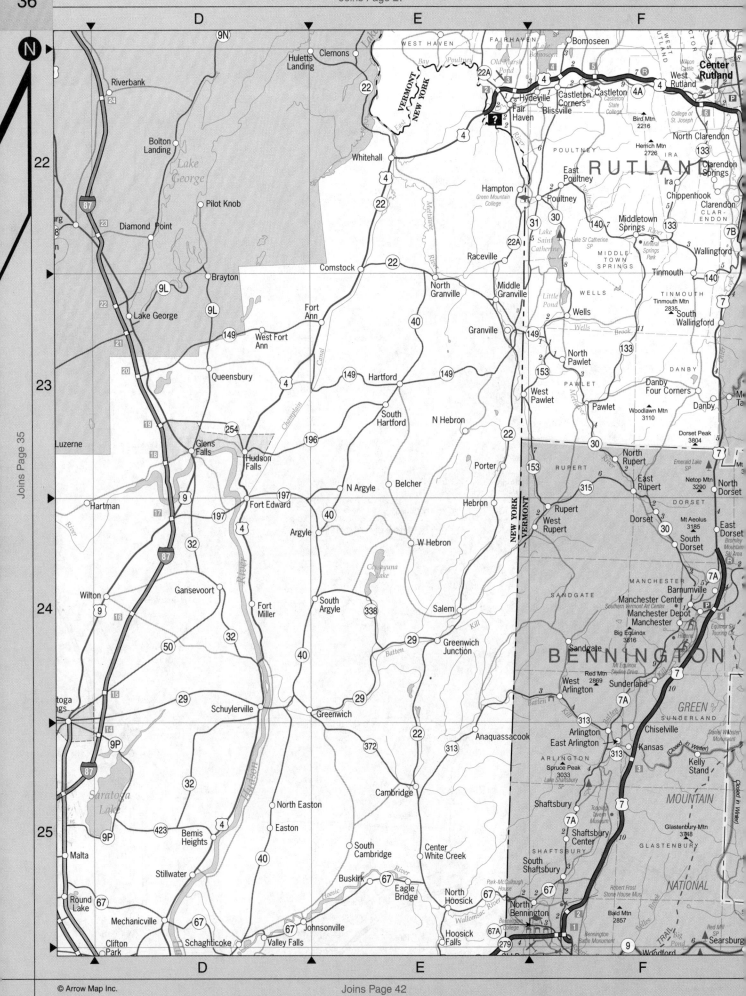

Joins Page 35

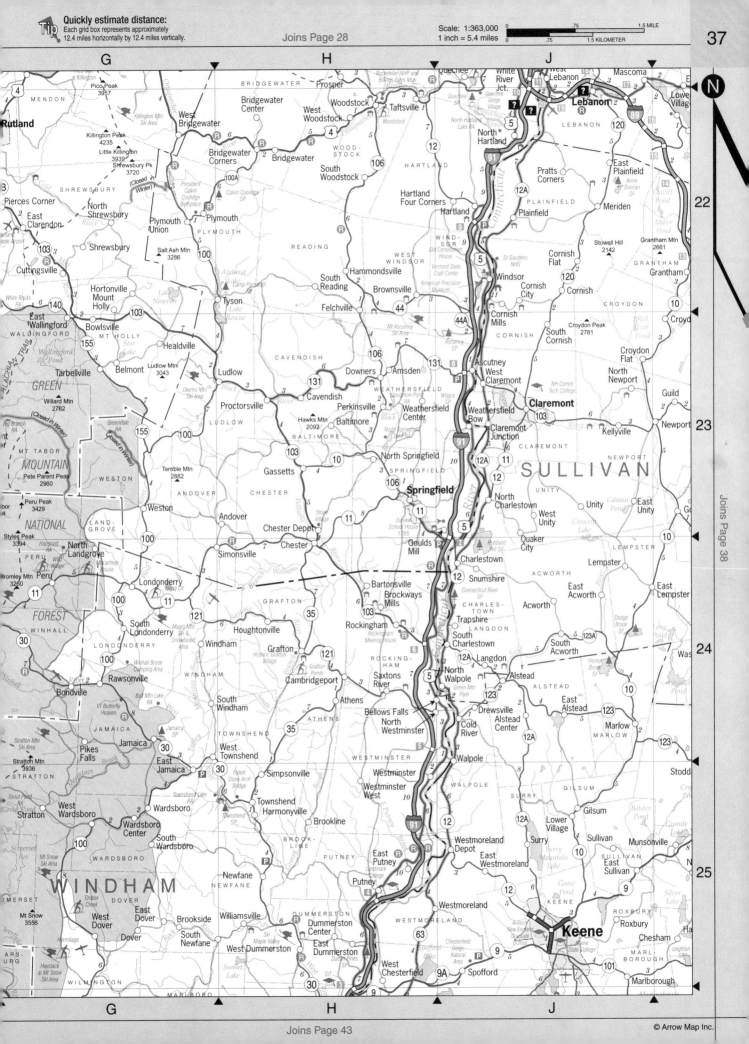

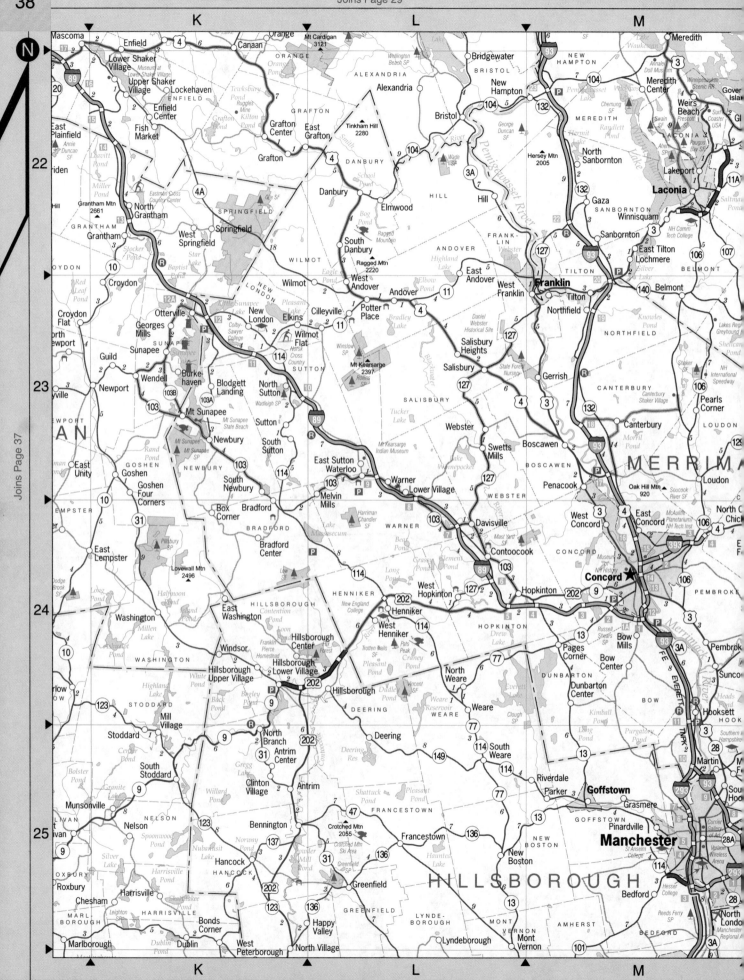

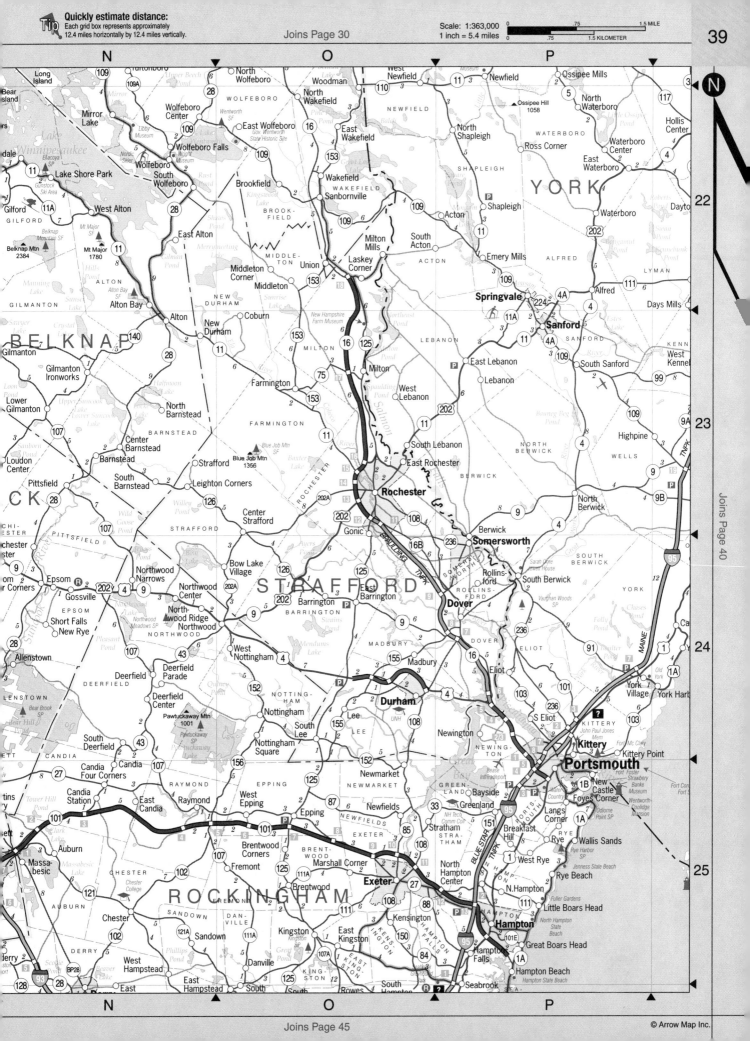

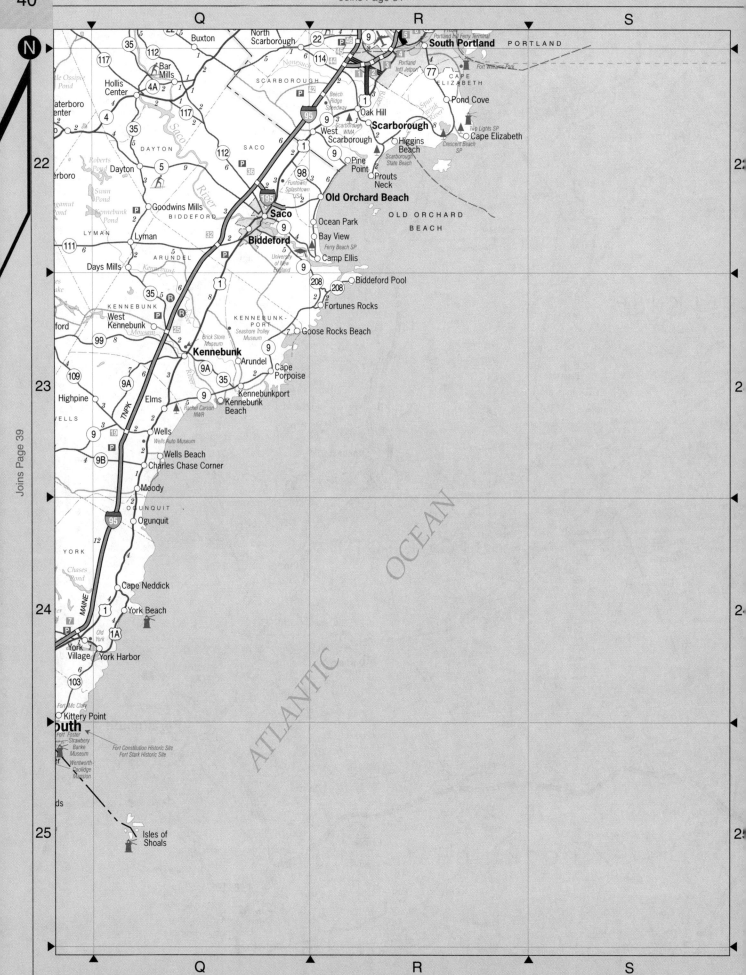

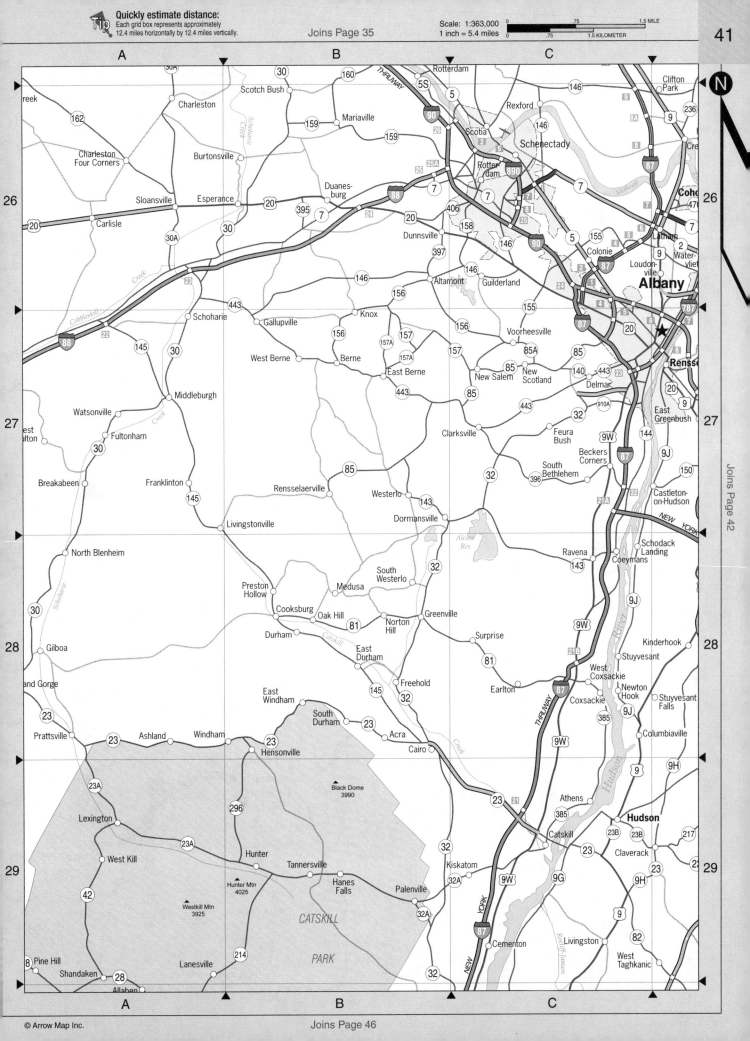

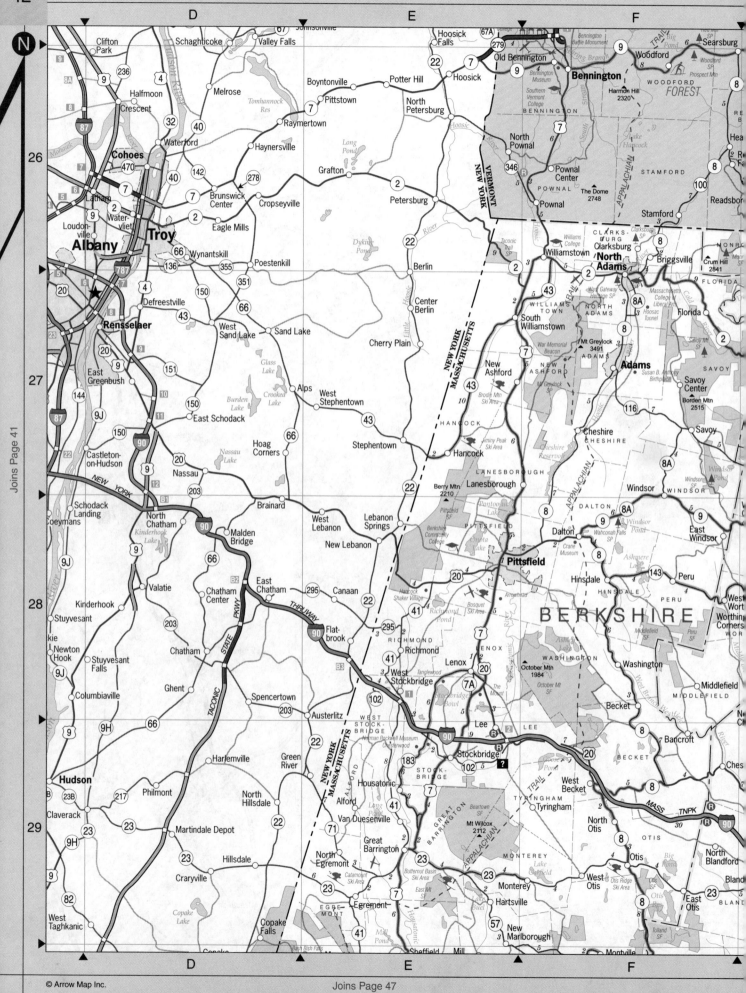

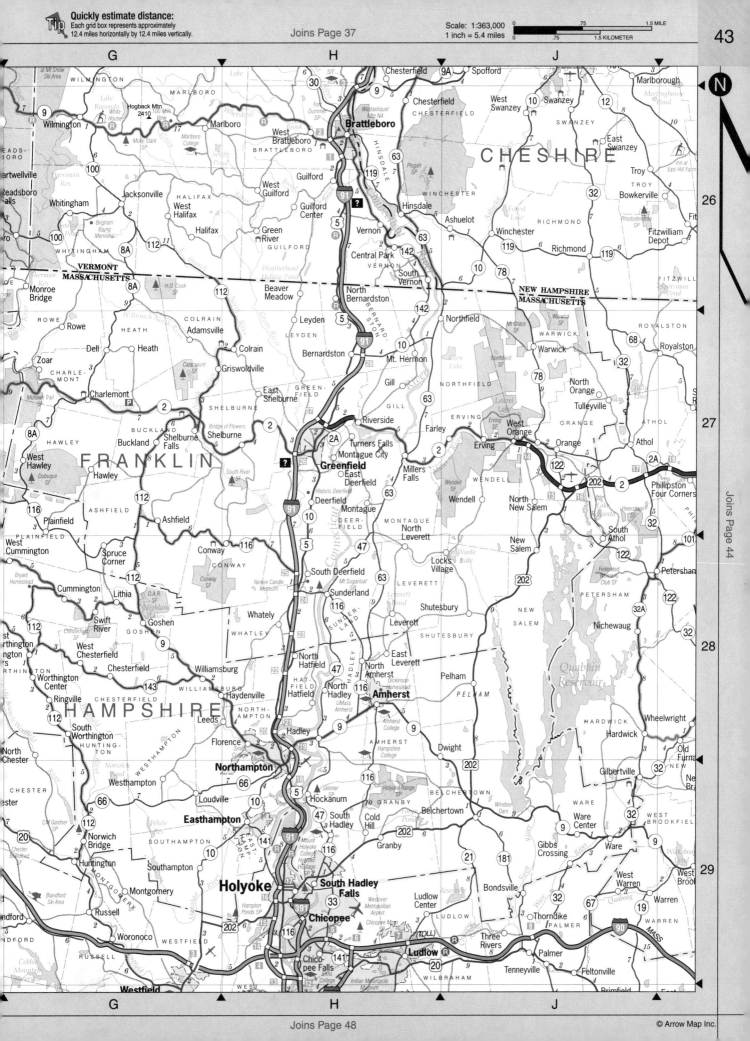

Quickly estimate distance:
Each grid box represents approximately
12.4 miles horizontally by 12.4 miles vertically.

Scale: 1:363,000
1 inch = 5.4 miles

.75   1.5 MILE
.75   1.5 KILOMETER

G H J

N

CHESHIRE

FRANKLIN

HAMPSHIRE

VERMONT
MASSACHUSETTS

NEW HAMPSHIRE
MASSACHUSETTS

Brattleboro
Greenfield
Amherst
Northampton
Easthampton
Holyoke
Chicopee
Westfield

Joins Page 44

© Arrow Map Inc.

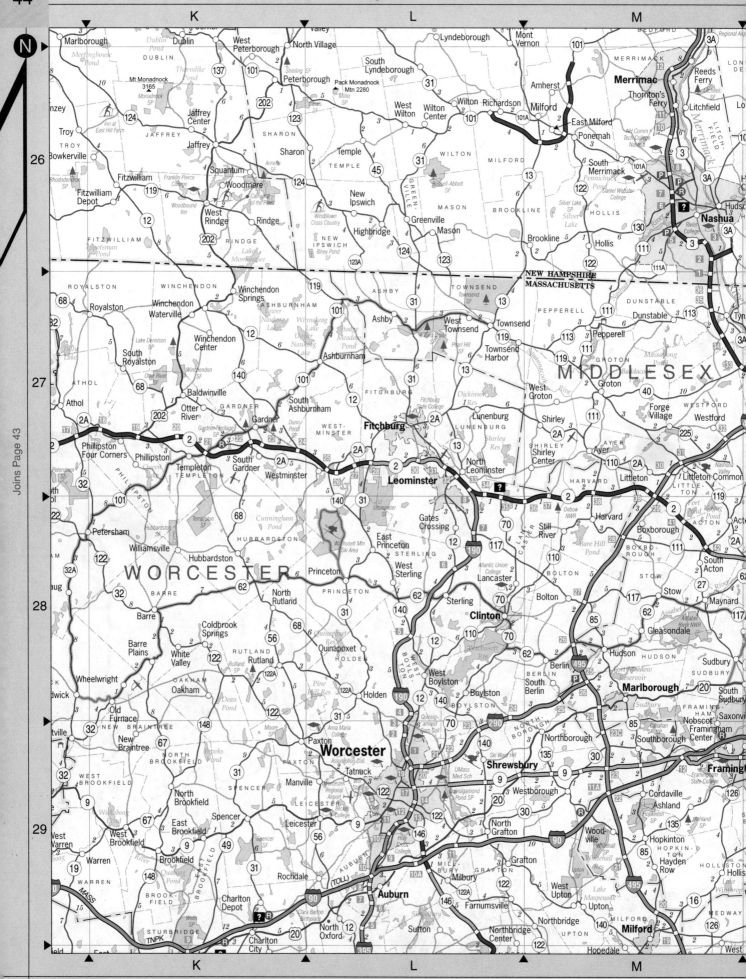

Quickly estimate distance:
Each grid box represents approximately
12.4 miles horizontally by 12.4 miles vertically.

Scale: 1:363,000
1 inch = 5.4 miles

© Arrow Map Inc.

N

A   B   C

30

31

32

33

Shandaken
Big Indian
Allaben
28
Phoenicia
Oliverea
Panther Mtn 3760
Mount Tremper
212
Doubletop Mtn 3905
Boiceville
Slide Mtn 4204
Woodstock
375
West Hurley
28
CATSKILL
28
28A
Stony Hollow
PARK
Ashokan Reservoir
Hurley
Olive Bridge
Esopus
Creek
Kingston
213
209
19
87
32
Rosendale
Kripplebush
213
Rifton
High Falls
Creek
213
32
Kerhonkson
209
Rondout
55
Wawarsing
Napanoch
44
West Park
299
New Paltz
18
Lloyd
299
52
Ellenville
208
Highland
44
Clintondale
44
52
Modena
52
32
Summitville
209
Lattintown
Pine Bush
Plattekill
87
Wurtsboro
116
302
Wallkill
300
Marlboro
115
17
52
208
New Hamburg
118
Bullville
17K
Walden
Middle Hope
9W
119
Montgomery
Coldenham
6
17
8
32
211
5
84
32
Newburgh
Beacon
17M
Maybrook
207
New Windsor
9D
120
208
94
Middletown
84
121
4
Wallkill
Vails Gate
Cornwall-on-Hudson
17
207
94
Salisbury Mills
Cornwall
218
301
Goshen
Washingtonville
Mountainville
9W
Cold Spring
Garrison
403
17A
208
32
Chester
126
6
218
94
17M
17
130
Highland Falls
293
87
Central Valley

Saugerties
32
212
Clermont
9
Tivoli
Glasco
9G
Upper Red Hook
Elizaville
20
212
Annandale-on-Hudson
Jackson Corners
9W
32
199
Red Hook
Rock City
199
Rhinebeck
308
199
Lafaye
9
Rhinecliff
Silver Lake
Kingston
Port Ewen
Eddyville
9
St Remy
9G
Ulster Park
Staatsburg
Long Pond
Pleasant Plains
Clinton Hollow
Esopus
Salt Point
Hyde Park
82
East Park
Washington Hollow
9W
9
Pleasant Valley
44
9G
115
Rochdale
Verbank
Poughkeepsie
82
Moores Mills
376
55
Milton
Billings
Red Oaks Mill
55
376
82
Wappingers Falls
Hopewell Junction
Stormville
Hughsonville
376
21
9D
9
East Fishkill
52
Fishkill
16
11
84
15
52
10
52
12
13
Pecksville
9
TRAIL
84
APPALACHIAN
Kent Cliffs
301
West Branch Res
Lake Mahopac
6N
301
6
Croton
Mahopac
PKWY
Hudson River
Wappinger
Kill
TACONIC STATE PKWY
THRUWAY
Wallkill River

Quickly estimate distance:
Each grid box represents approximately 12.4 miles horizontally by 12.4 miles vertically.

Scale: 1:363,000
1 inch = 5.4 miles

0 .75 1.5 MILE
0 .75 1.5 KILOMETER

N

Joins Page 48

HAMPD

MASSACHUSETTS
CONNECTICUT

NEW YORK
CONNECTICUT

LITCHFIELD

NEW HAVE

Copake, West Copake, Ancram, Ancramdale, Pine Plains, Bangall, Stanfordville, Millbrook, South Millbrook, Amenia, Amenia Union, Lithgow, Wassaic, Mabbettsville, Dover Plains, Clove, Wingdale, Poughquag, Stonehouse, Pawling, Holmes, Patterson, Towners, Kent Corners, Carmel, Tilly Foster, Brewster

Falls, Mount Washington, Alander Mtn 2239, Mt Everett 2602, Joyceville, Taconic, Salisbury, Lakeville, Amesville, Falls Village, Sharon, West Cornwall, Cornwall Center, Ellsworth, Cornwall Bridge, North Kent, Macedonia, Flanders, Kent Furnace, Kent, South Kent, Bulls Bridge, Gaylordsville, Upper Merryall, New Preston, Marbledale, Lower Merryall, Northville, Boardman Bridge, Park Lane, New Milford, Sherman, Roxbury Station, Roxbury, Bridgewater, New Fairfield, Knollcrest, Candlewood Isle, Candlewood Shores, Brookfield, Brookfield Center, Mill Plain, New Fairfield

Sheffield, Mill River, Konpapot, Ashley Falls, Clayton, Sodom, Canaan, Canaan Valley, North Canaan, East Canaan, West Canaan, Huntsville, South Canaan, Lower City, South Norfolk, Cornwall Hollow, Cornwall, Goshen, West Goshen, Warren, Milton, Litchfield, Bantam, Woodville, Lakeside, Romford, Morris, East Morris, Northfield, Washington, Washington Depot, Bethlehem, Watertown, Minortown, Woodbury, North Woodbury, Hotchkissville, Roxbury Falls, Southbury, White Oaks, South Britain, Sandy Hook, Newtown, Dodgingtown, Berkshire, Stevenson, Botsford, East Village, Huntington

New Marlborough, Montville, New Boston, Sandisfield, Southfield, Tolland, West Granville, North Colebrook, Colebrook, Robertsville, Norfolk, North Norfolk, West Norfolk, Winchester Center, Newfield, Burrville, Drakeville, Wrightville, West Torrington, Torrington, Torringford, Harwinton, East Litchfield, Harwinton, Campville, Plymouth, Thomaston, Reynolds Bridge, Hancock, Greystone, Oakville, Watertown, Oronoke, Middlebury, Pomperaug, Southford, Quaker Farms, Oxford, Beacon Falls, Seymour, Riverside, Woodbridge, Augerville, Mount Carmel, Bethany, Hamden, Cheshire, Prospect, Naugatuck, Union City, Straitsville, Millville, Bradleyville, Waterville, Marion, Wolcott, East Plymouth, Edgewood, Terryville, Pequabuck, Bristol, Burlington, Unionville, Whigville, Nepaug, Bakersville, Collinsville, Pine Meadow, New Hartford, Pleasant Valley, Riverton, West Hartland, East Hartland, Hartland, Waterbury

West Granville, Granville SF, Winchester, Goshen

© Arrow Map Inc.

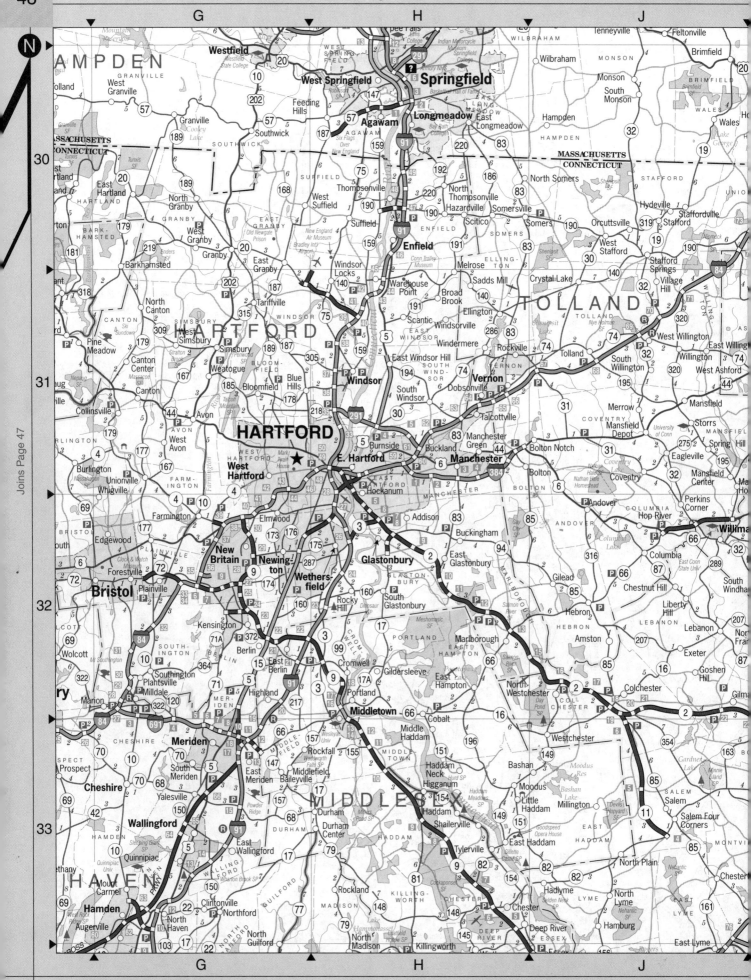

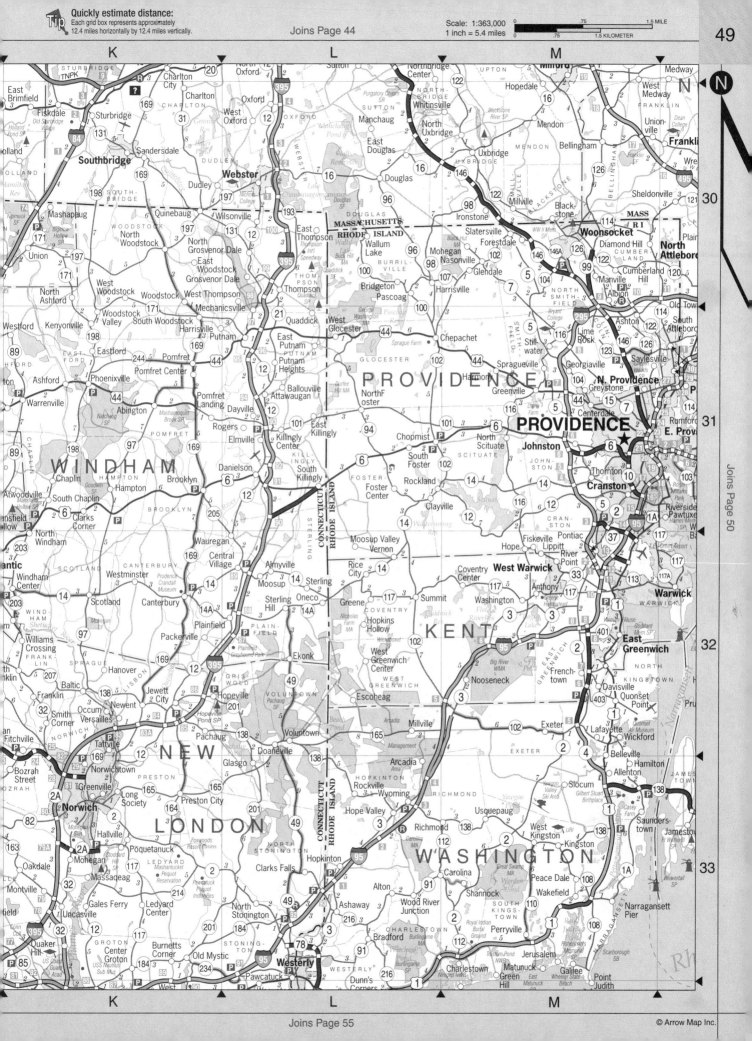

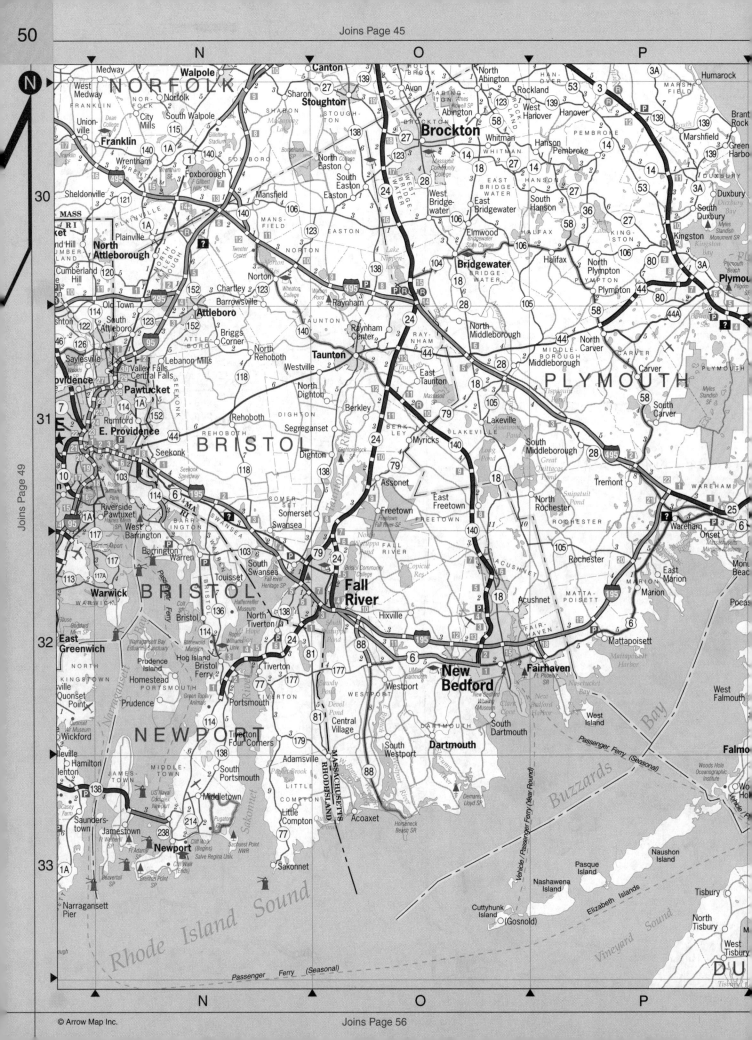

Joins Page 49

Quickly estimate distance:
Each grid box represents approximately
12.4 miles horizontally by 12.4 miles vertically.

Scale: 1:363,000
1 inch = 5.4 miles

0   .75   1.5 MILE
0   .75   1.5 KILOMETER

N

CAPE COD

PROVINCETOWN
6
Provincetown
6A
North Truro
6A
TRURO
Truro
NATIONAL

Passenger Ferry (Seasonal)

WELLFLEET
Wellfleet
South Wellfleet

SEASHORE

Cape Cod

Manomet Bluffs
Manomet

Plimoth Plantation

Cape Cod Bay

North Eastham

EASTHAM

3
3A

Ellisville SP
Ellisville

Cedarville

Bournedale

Sagamore

Sandwich

East Sandwich

6A

Eastham

East Brewster

Nickerson SP

Brewster

BREWSTER

Orleans

East Orleans

ORLEANS

East Dennis

West Brewster

124 137

Dennis

DENNIS

134

6

Cummaquid

Barnstable

Yarmouth Port

Yarmouth

South Dennis

11

39

Pleasant Bay

North Chatham

28

CHATHAM

Chatham

BARNSTABLE

SANDWICH

Camp Edwards (Military Reservation)

130

Forestdale

149

132

Mashpee

Marstons Mills

Cape Cod Community College

South Yarmouth

YARMOUTH

West Yarmouth

Dennis Port

28

Harwich Port

HARWICH

39

Harwich

South Chatham

Sequetucket Harbor

Buzzards Bay

Bourne

28

151

Centerville

Osterville

Cotuit

Hyannis

Hyannis Port

West Dennis

Craigville Beach

Lewis Bay

MASHPEE

Waquoit Village

New Seabury

FALMOUTH

East Falmouth

Teaticket

Falmouth Heights

South Cape Beach SP

Waquoit Bay Research Reserve

Monomoy NWR

Monomoy Island

Nantucket Sound

Passenger Ferry (Seasonal)

Vehicle Passenger Ferry (Seasonal)

Passenger Ferry (Year-Round)

Passenger Ferry (Seasonal)

Vineyard Haven

Oak Bluffs

Edgartown

Chappaquiddick Island

Manuell Corellius SP

Nantucket NWR

KES

© Arrow Ma

N

A   B   C

34

35

36

37

Florida
Warwick
94
Greenwood Lake
210
17A
NEW YORK
NEW JERSEY
Tuxedo Park
17
Sloatsburg
West Milford
Ringwood
Wanaque Res
Greenwood Lake

APPALACHIAN TRAIL
APPALACHIAN TRAIL

17M
17
130
87
Monroe
Central Valley
16
17
8
NEW YORK STATE

PALISADES
INTERSTATE
PARK
Lake Sebago
Lake Welch
15
13
12
202
PALISADES INTERSTATE

Ft Montgomery
9D
6
17
202
18
6
9
Tomkins Cove
16
Stony Point
129
West Haverstraw
Haverstraw
9W
Lake DeForest
304
New City
306
45
303
Spring Valley
13
12
Monsey
Suffern
59
287
66
NEW YORK NEW JERSEY
14A
14
59
9
Nanuet
304
West Nyack
303
Pearl River
172
Orangeburg
5
Lake Tappan Res
Tappan
Westwood
Harrington Park
Closter
Dumont
9W
Oradell

Shrub Oak
118
Somer
6
132
STATE
PKWY
Peekskill
202
Buchanan
New Croton Res
Croton-On-Hudson
134
Ossining
9A
133
9
117
448
Nyack
59
11
North Tarrytown
10
287
9
1
Dobbs Ferry
SAW MILL RIVER
7A
SPRAIN
BK
PKWY

118
202
139
10
Amawalk
35
Yorktown Heights
100
Katonah
Croton Res
Kitch-awan
Mt Kisco
172
100
133
120
Chappaqua
117
Pleasantville
Armonk
120
128
684
Kensico Res
22
2
120
White Plains
127
20
287
95
1
Harris
Mamaroneck
Larchmont
New Rochelle
Pelham Manor
15
14

Upper Saddle River
Ramsey
Wyckoff
17
Ho-Ho-Kus
168
GARDEN STATE PKWY
Oakland
202
59
Wanaque
57
58
287
23
Butler
55
53
202
52
Pompton Lakes
208
Ridgewood
Glen Rock
153
Haledon
Lincoln Park
202
Wayne
Fair Lawn
47
Towaco
53
PATERSON
57
Passaic River
80
Little Falls
46
Clifton
157
Caldwell
153
Cedar Grove
Verona
23
Montclair
Bloomfield
7
Livingston
280
10
East Orange
12
Kearny
Irvington
124
280
144
143
NEWARK
57
1
9
24
124
48
49
78
Springfield
Union
22
78
Mountainside
140
82
439
140
Elizabeth
22
Cranford
137
28
Westfield
Clark
136
Roselle
27
Plainfield
135
Linden
1
95
9
Rahway
27
12

4
161
Paramus
Bergenfield
4
Hackensack
64
Teaneck
46
80
Englewood
68
Fort Lee
2A
Rutherford
17
18
Se-caucus
16W
16E
17
NEW JERSEY TNPK
Union City
Hoboken
Jersey City
14C
78
14B
14A
440
Bayonne
New York Bay
STATEN ISLAND
440
13A
Newark Int'l Airport
15W
9A
9
1
Kill Van Kull
278
SHORE
16
7

Yonkers
Mt Vernon
BRONX RIVER PKWY
9
95
4B
4A
278
6B
HENRY HUDSON DRIVE
PALISADES INT PKWY
MANHATTAN
FDR DRIVE
East River
Rikers Island
La Guardia Airport
3
13
678
295
25A
36
25A
Long Island
NEW YORK
BROOKLYN
27
17
Jamaica Bay
J.F.K. Int'l Airport
SHORE PKWY

Sands Point
Port Washington
Kings Point
Great Neck
Manhasset
Little Neck Bay
Manhasset Bay
25A
Elmont
24
25
Valley Str
23B
Roc Ce
Crot

© Arrow Map Inc.

A   B   C

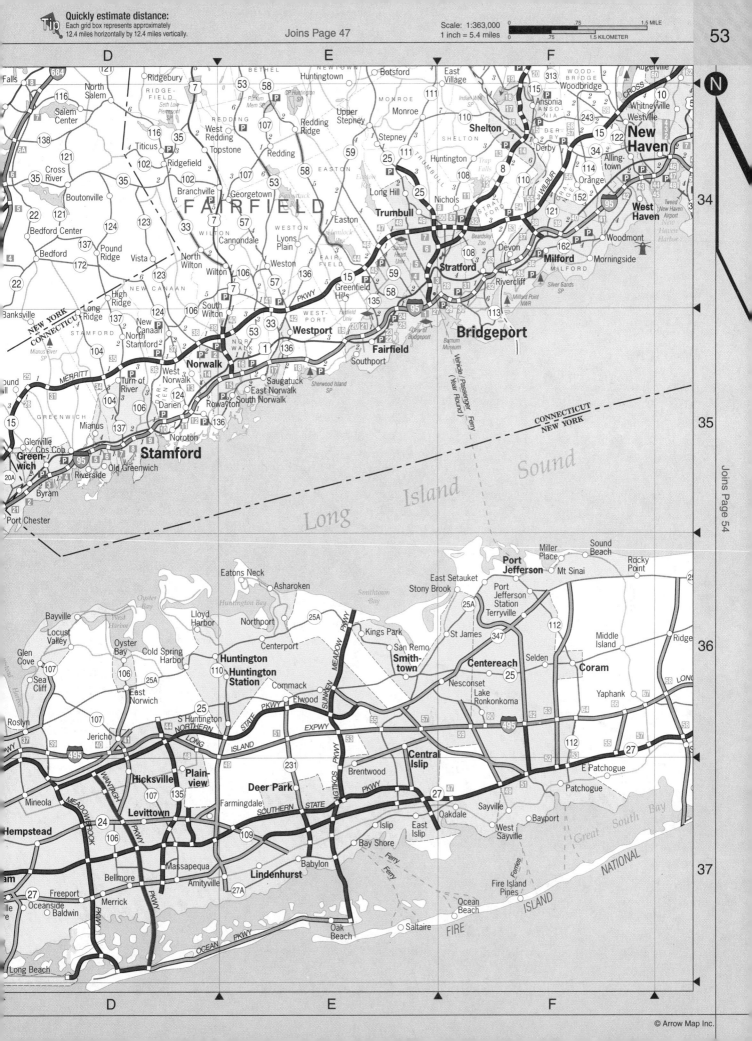

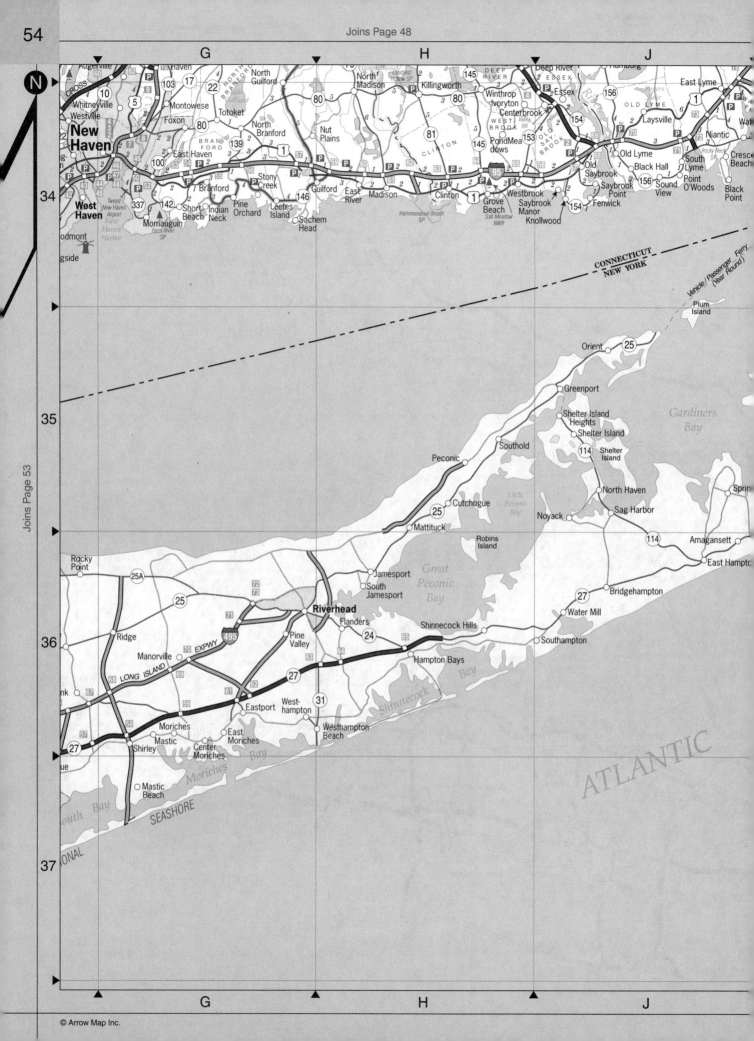

Quickly estimate distance:
Each grid box represents approximately
12.4 miles horizontally by 12.4 miles vertically.

Scale: 1:363,000
1 inch = 5.4 miles

N   O   P

Joins Page 55

N

Passenger   Ferry   (Seasonal)

D U

Menemsha

Aquinnah
(Gay Head)

Chilmark

Tisbury
Great Pond

Menemsha
Pond

Squibnocket
Pond

Nomans
Land

34

ATLANTIC

35

36

37

N   O   P

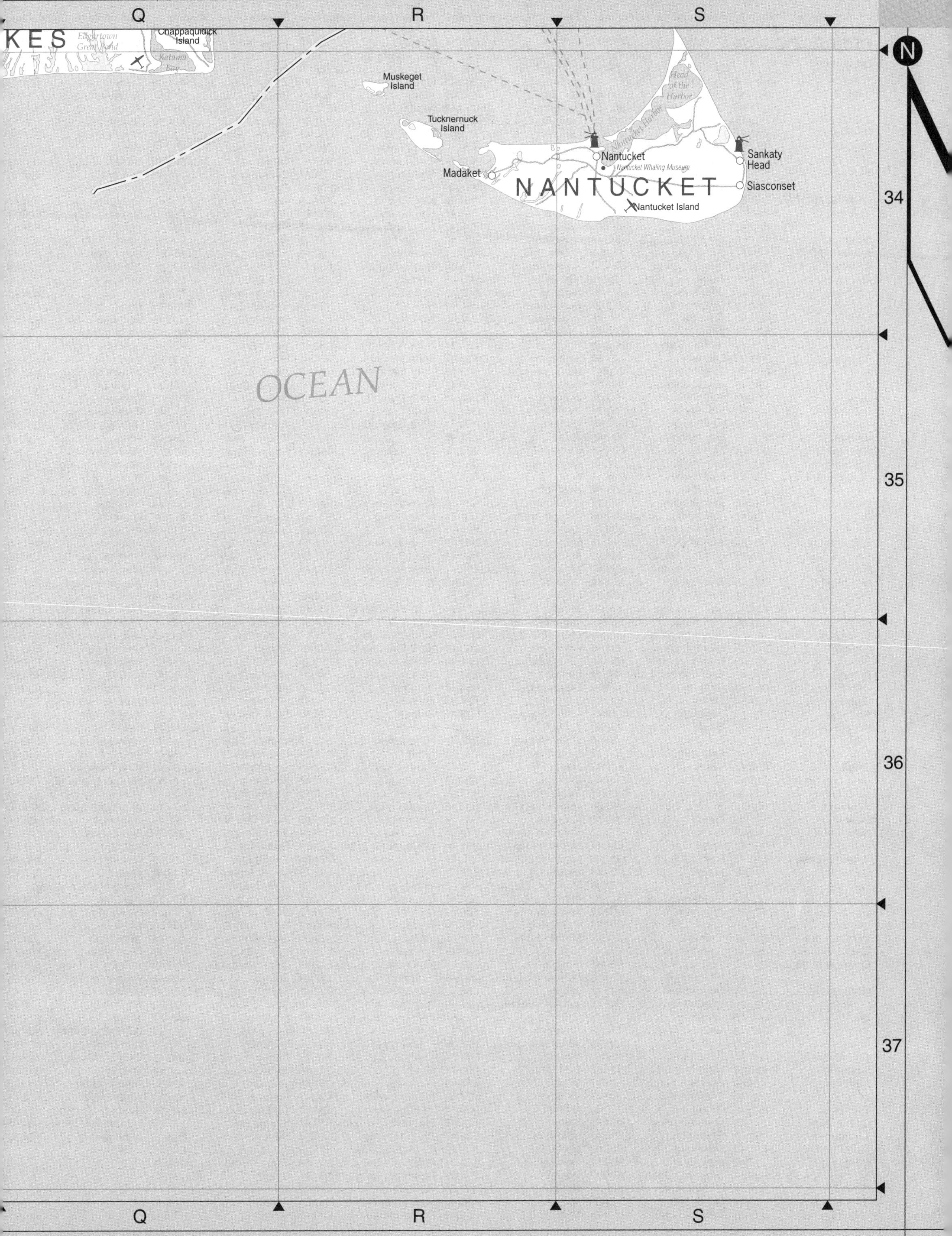

Quickly estimate distance:
Each grid box represents approximately
12.4 miles horizontally by 12.4 miles vertically.

Scale: 1:363,000
1 inch = 5.4 miles

0   .75   1.5 MILE
0   .75   1.5 KILOMETER

Q   R   S

N

KES
Edgartown
Great Pond
Chappaquidick
Island

Katama
Bay

Muskeget
Island

Tucknernuck
Island

34

Head
of the
Harbor

Nantucket Harbor

Nantucket

Sankaty
Head

Madaket

Nantucket Whaling Museum

Siasconset

N A N T U C K E T

Nantucket Island

OCEAN

35

36

37

Q   R   S

Connecticut

Feature Name Grid:Page

MASSACHUSETTS

Connecticut to New Hampshire

Feature Name	Grid:Page
Strawbery Banke Museum	P25:39
Tenney Mountain Ski Area	L21:29
The Balsams/Wilderness Ski Area	N15:20
The Basin	L19:29
The Flume	L19:29
University of New Hampshire	O24:39
Waterville Valley Ski Area	M20:29
Wentworth-Coolidge Mansion	P25:39
Whaleback Ski Area	J22:37
Whales Tale Waterpark	L19:29
White Mountain National Forest	M18:29
Wildcat Mountain Ski Area	N18:30
Winnipesaukee Scenic Railroad	M22:38
Wright Museum	N22:39

RHODE ISLAND

Feature Name	Grid:Page
Blithewold Mansion	N32:50
Bryant College	M31:49
Casey Farm	M33:49
Cliff Walk	N33:50
Dame Farm	M31:49
Gilbert Stuart Birthplace	M33:49
Green Topiary Animals	N32:50
Greene Homestead	M32:49
Haffenreffer Museum	N32:50
Purgatory Chasm	N33:50
Quonset Air Museum	M32:49
Roger Williams Park Zoo	N31:50
Roger Williams University	N32:50
Royal Indian Burial Ground	M33:49
Salve Regina University	N33:50
Sprague Farm	L31:49
T F Green Airport	M32:49
University of Rhode Island	M33:49
U S Naval Complex (Newport)	N33:50
Varnum House Museum	M32:49
Wheeler State Beach	M33:49
Yawgoo Valley Ski Area	M33:49

VERMONT

Feature Name	Grid:Page
American Precision Museum	H22:37
Appalachian Trail	G21:28-F26:42
Bayley-Hazen Military Road Monument	J17:18
Ben & Jerry's Ice Cream Factory	G18:28
Bennington Battle Monument Historic Site	F25:36
Bennington College	E25:36
Bennington Museum	F26:42
Big Falls	J14:18
Billings Farm Museum	H21:28
Bingham Falls	G17:18
Bolton Valley Ski Area	G17:18
Bread and Puppet Museum	J16:18
Brigham Young Memorial	G26:43
Bromley Mountain Ski Area	F24:36
Brookfield Gulf	H19:28
Burke Mountain Ski Area	L16:19
Burke Mountain Toll Road	L17:19
Burlington International Airport	F17:17
Burlington College	E17:17
Cabot Creamery	J17:18
Castleton State College	F22:36
Champlain College	E17:17
Cochran Ski Area	F18:27
College of St Joseph	F22:36
Daniel Webster Monument	F25:36
Equinox Ski Touring Center	F24:36
Ethan Allen Homestead	E17:17
Eureka School House (1785)	H23:37
Fairbanks Museum & Planetarium	K17:19
Follett Stone Arch Bridge	H25:37
Goddard College	J18:28
Green Mountain College	E22:36
Green Mountain Flyer	J24:37
Green Mountain National Forest	F19:27, F24:36
Haystack at Mt. Snow Ski Area	G25:37
Hildene	F24:36
Hubbardton Gulf	F21:27
Hubbarton Battle Monument & Museum	F21:27
Jay Peak Ski Area	H15:18
Johnson State College	H16:18
Joseph Smith Monument	H20:28
Justin Smith Morrill Homestead	J20:28
Kents Museum	H18:28
Killington Mountain Ski Area	G22:37
Landmark College	H25:37
Lyndon Outing Club Ski Area	K17:19
Lyndon State College	K17:19
Mad River Glen Ski Area	G18:28
Magic Mountain Ski & Snowboard Area	G24:37
Marlboro College	G26:43
Middlebury College Snow Bowl	F20:27
Middlebury College	F19:27
Mineral Springs Park	F22:36
Montshire Museum of Science	J21:28
Morgan Horse Farm	F19:27
Moss Glen Falls	H17:18
Mount Independence State Historic Site	E21:27
Mt Ascutney Ski Area	H23:37
Mt Equinox Skyline Drive	F24:36
Mt Snow Ski Area	G25:37
Norwich University Ski Area	H19:28
Norwich University	H19:28
Okemo Mountain Ski Area	G23:37
Old Constitution House	J22:37
Old Stone House	K15:19
100 Mile View	G26:43
Park-McCullough House	E25:36
Pico Mountain at Killington	G21:28
President Calvin Coolidge Birthplace	G22:37
President Chester Arthur Birthplace	G15:18
Quechee Gorge	J22:37
Rockingham Meeting House	H24:37
Rock of Ages Quarries	H19:28
Rokeby	F18:27
Royal Lipizzan Stallions of Austria	E15:17
Rutland State Airport	G22:37
Samuel DeChamplain Statue	E15:17
Shelburne Farms	E17:17
Shelburne Museum	E18:27
Sheldon Museum	F20:27
Ski Maple Valley	H25:37
Smugglers Notch Ski Area	G17:18
Southern Vermont Art Center	F24:36
Southern Vermont College	F26:42
St Anne Shrine	E15:17
St Michaels College	F17:17
Sterling College	J16:18
Stone Village	H23:37
Stowe Mountain Resort	G17:18
Stowe Mountain Toll Road	G17:18
Stratton Mountain Ski Area	G24:37
Sugarbush North Ski Area	G19:28
Sugarbush Valley Ski Area	G19:28
Suicide Six Ski Area	H21:28
Texas Falls	G20:28
Topping Tavern Museum	F25:36
University of Vermont	F17:17
Vermont Law School	H20:28
Vermont Marble Exhibit	F21:27
Vermont State Craft Center (Frog Hollow)	F20:27
Vermont State Craft Center (Windsor)	J22:37
Vermont Technical College	H20:28
William Scott Monument	J18:28
Williamstown Gulf	H19:28
Woodbury College	H18:28

Public Recreation Areas

CONNECTICUT

Feature Name	Grid:Page	Community	Phone
Algonquin State Forest	F30:47	Colebrook	
American Legion State Forest	F30:47	Barkhamsted	
Bigelow Hollow State Park	K30:49	Union	(860) 928-9200
Black Rock State Park	F32:47	Thomaston	(860) 677-1819
Bluff Point State Park	K34:55	Groton	
Burr Pond State Park	F31:47	Torrington	(860) 482-1817
Campbell Falls State Park	F30:47	Norfolk	
Chatfield Hollow State Park	H33:48	Killingworth	(860) 663-2030
Cockaponset State Forest	H33:48	Chester, Haddam	(860) 345-8521
Collis P Huntington State Park	E34:53	Redding	
Day Pond State Park	J32:48	Colchester	
Dennis Hill State Park	F30:47	Norfolk	
Devils Hopyard State Park	J33:48	East Haddam	(860) 873-8566
Dinosaur State Park	H32:48	Rocky Hill	(860) 529-5816
Enders State Forest	G30:48	Granby	
Farm River State Park	G34:54	East Haven	
Fort Griswold State Park	K34:55	Groton	
Fort Trumbull State Park	K34:55	New London	(860) 445-1729
Gay City State Park	H32:48	Hebron	
Gillette Castle State Park	H33:48	East Haddam	(860) 526-2336
Goodwin State Forest	K31:49	Hampton	
Haddam Meadows State Park	H33:48	Haddam	
Haley Farm State Park	K34:55	Groton	
Hammonasset Beach State Park	H34:54	Madison	(203) 245-2785
Harkness Memorial State Park	K34:55	Waterford	(860) 443-5725
Haystack Mountain State Park	E30:47	Norfolk	
Hopeville Pond State Park	K32:49	Griswold	(860) 376-2920
Housatonic Meadows State Park	E31:47	Cornwall	
Housatonic State Forest	E30:47, E31:47	Canaan, Cornwall	
Hurd State Park	H33:48	Haddam	
Indian Well State Park	F34:53	Shelton	
Kent Falls State Park	E31:47	Kent	
Kettletown State Park	E33:47	Oxford	
Lake Waramaug State Park	E32:47	Kent	(860) 868-2592
Macedonia Brook State Park	D31:47	Kent	(860) 927-3238
Mansfield Hollow State Park	K31:49	Mansfield	(860) 928-6121
Mashamoquet Brook State Park	K31:49	Pomfret	(860) 928-6121
Massacoe State Forest	G30:48	Canton, Simsbury	
Mattatuck State Forest	F32:47	Litchfield, Plymouth, Waterbury	
Meshomasic State Forest	H32:48	Portland, Hampton	
Mianus River State Park	D35:53	Greenwich	
Milford Point National Wildlife Refuge	F34:53	Milford	(860) 339-2513
Millers Pond State Park	H33:48	Haddam	
Minetto State Park	F31:47	Torrington	
Minnie Island State Park	J33:48	Salem	
Mohawk Mountain State Park	E31:47	Cornwall	(860) 927-3238
Mohawk State Forest	E31:47	Cornwall, Goshen	
Mohegan State Forest	K32:49	Scotland	
Mount Riga State Park	E30:47	Salisbury	
Mount Tom State Park	E32:47	Washington	
Nassahegan State Forest	F31:47	Burlington	
Natchaug State Forest	K31:49	Eastford	(860) 928-6121
Nathan Hale State Forest	J31:49	Andover, Coventry	
Naugatuck State Forest	F33:47	Beacon Falls	
Nehantic State Forest	J33:48	East Lyme	
Nepaug State Forest	F31:47	New Hartford	
Nipmuck State Forest	J30:48, K30:49	Union	
Nye Holman State Forest	J31:49	Tolland	
Osbornedale State Park	F33:47	Ansonia	(203) 735-4311
Pachaug State Forest	L32:49	Griswold, Voluntown	(860) 376-2920
Paugnut State Forest	F31:47	Torrington	
Paugusset State Forest	E33:47	Newtown	
Penwood State Park	G30:48	Bloomfield	(860) 242-1158
Peoples State Forest	F30:47	Barkhamsted	(860) 379-2469
Platt Hill State Park	F31:47	Winchester	
Pootatuck State Forest	D33:47	Sherman	
Putnam Memorial State Park	E34:53	Redding	(203) 797-4165
Quaddick State Forest	L30:49	Thompson	
Quaddick State Park	L30:49	Thompson	(860) 928-9200
Rocky Glen State Park	E33:47	Newtown	
Rocky Neck State Park	J34:54	East Lyme	(860) 739-5471
Salmon River State Forest	H32:48	Marlborough, Colechester	(860) 295-9523
Salt Meadow National Wildlife Refuge	H34:54	Westbrook	(860) 339-2513
Selden Neck State Park	J33:48	Lyme	
Seth Low Pierrepont State Park	D34:53	Ridgefield	
Shenipsit State Forest	J30:48	Ellington, Stafford	(860) 684-3430
Sherwood Island State Park	E35:53	Westport	(203) 226-6983
Silver Sands State Park	F34:53	Milford	
Sleeping Giant State Park	G33:48	Hamden	(203) 789-7498
Southford Falls State Park	F33:47	Oxford	(203) 264-5169
Squantz Pond State Park	D33:47	New Fairfield	(203) 797-4165
Stoddard Hill State Park	K33:49	Preston	
Stratton Brook State Park	G30:48	Simsbury	
Talcott Mountain State Park	G30:48	Bloomfield	
Topsmead State Forest	F31:47	Litchfield	(203) 567-5694
Tunxis State Forest	F30:47, G30:48	Hartland, Barkhamsted	
Wadsworth Falls State Park	G33:48	Middlefield	(860) 663-2030
West Rock Ridge State Park	F33:47	Hamden	
Wharton Brook State Park	G33:48	North Haven	
Wyantenock State Forest	E31:47	Kent	

Public Recreation Areas

Feature Name	Grid:Page	Community	Phone

MAINE

Feature Name	Grid:Page	Community	Phone
Acadia National Park	Z18:34, X19:33	Hancock, Knox County	(207) 288-3338
Allagash Wilderness Waterway	KK18,GG17	Aroostook, Piscataquis County	
			(207) 695-3721
Aroostook State Park	AA6:9	Presque Isle	(207) 768-8341
Baxter State Park	W9:8	Piscataquis County	(207) 723-5140
Bigelow Preserve	R13:11	Somerset, Franklin Counties	
			(207) 778-8231
Birch Point State Park	W19:33	Owls Head	(207) 768-8341
Bradbury Mountain State Park	R20:31	Pownal	(207) 688-4712
Camden Hills State Park	W18:33	Camden	(207) 236-3109
Cobscook Bay State Park	DD15:25	Dennysville	(207) 726-4412
Crescent Beach State Park	R22:40	Cape Elizabeth	(207) 767-3625
Damariscotta Lake State Park	U19:32	Jefferson	(207) 549-7600
Ferry Beach State Park	Q22:40	Saco	(207) 283-0067
Fort Point State Park	W17:23	Stockton Springs	(207) 596-2253
Grafton Notch State Park	O16:20	Newry	(207) 824-2912
Holbrook Island Sanctuary	X18:33	Brooksville	(207) 326-4012
Lake St.George State Park	U17:22	Liberty	(207) 589-4255
Lamoine State Park	Z17:24	Lamoine	(207) 667-4778
Lily Bay State Park	U11:12	Beaver Cove	(207) 695-2700
Moose Point State Park	W17:23	Searsport	(207) 548-2882
Moosehorn National Wildlife Refuge	CC14:25 DD15:25		
		Washington County	(207) 454-3521
Mount Blue State Park	Q16:21	Weld	(207) 585-2261
Nahmakanta Public Reserve Lands	DV17:22	Piscataquis County	(207) 827-5936
Peacock Beach State Park	J19:28	Richmond	(207) 582-2813
Peaks-Kenny State Park	V13:12	Dover-Foxcroft	(207) 564-2003
Petit Manan National Wildlife Refuge	AA17:24 CC16:25, E17:176		
		Washington County	(207)546-2124
Popham Beach State Park	T21:32	Phippsburg	(207) 389-1335
Quoddy Head State Park	EE15:25	Lubec	(207) 733-0911
Range Ponds State Park	R19:31	Poland	(207) 998-4104
Rachel Carson National Wildlife Refuge	Q23:40	Wells, Kennebunk	(207) 646-9266
Rangeley Lake State Park	P15:20	Rangeley	(207) 864-3838
Reid State Park	T21:32	Georgetown	(207) 371-2303
Roosevelt-Campobello International Park	EE15:25	Lubec, New Brunswick	(506)752-2922
Roque Bluffs State Park	CC16:25	Roque Bluffs	(207) 255-3475
Scarborough Beach Park	R22:40	Scarborough	(207) 657-2345
Scarborough Wildlife Management Area	Q22:40	Scarborough, Old Orchard Beach	(207) 657-2345
Sebago Lake State Park	Q20:31	Naples	(207) 693-6615
Shackford Head State Park	DD15:25	Eastport	(207) 941-4104
Steep Falls Wildlife Management Area	Q21:31	Standish, Baldwin	(207) 657-2345
Swan Island Wildlife Management Area	T19:32	Perkins Township	(207) 547-5322
Swan Lake State Park	W17:23	Swanville	(207) 799-5871
Vaughan Woods State Park	P24:39	South Berwick	(207) 384-5160
Warren Island State Park	W18:33	Islesboro	(207) 236-3109
White Mountain National Forest	O18:30	Oxford County	(207) 824-2134
Wolfe's Neck Woods State Park	S21:31	Freeport	(207) 624-6075

MASSACHUSETTS

Feature Name	Grid:Page	Community	Phone
Ames Nowell State Park	O30:50	Abington	(781) 857-1336
Appalachian Trail	E29:42-F27:42	Monterey, Cheshire	(413) 442-8928
Ashland State Park	M29:44	Ashland	(508) 435-4303
Bash Bish Falls State Park	D30:47	Mount Washington	(413) 528-0330
Beartown State Forest	E29:42	Monterey	(413) 528-0904
Blackstone River Heritage State Park	M30:49	Uxbridge	(508) 278-6486, (508) 278-7604
Blue Hills Reservation	O29:45	Milton	(617) 698-1802
Borderland State Park	N30:50	Easton	(508) 238-6566
Boston Harbor Islands State Park	O29:45	Boston	(617) 223-8666
Bradley Palmer State Park	O27:45	Topsfield	(978) 887-5931
Brimfield State Forest	J30:48	Brimfield	(413) 267-9687
Callahan State Park	M29:44	Framingham	(508) 653-9641
Campbell Falls State Forest	E30:47	New Marlborough	(413) 528-0904
Cape Cod National Seashore	S30:51	Eastham	(508) 255-3421
Catamount State Forest	G27:43	Colrain	(413) 339-5504
Chester-Blandford State Forest	G29:43	Chester	(413) 354-6347
Chesterfield State Forest	G28:43	Chesterfield	(413) 296-4729
Chicopee Memorial State Park	H29:43	Chicopee	(413) 594-9416
Clarksburg State Park	F26:42	Clarksburg	(413) 663-8469
CM Gardner State Park	G29:43	Huntington	(413) 354-6347
Cochituate State Park	N28:45	Wayland	(508) 653-9641
Conway State Forest	G28:43	Conway	(413) 268-7098
DAR State Forest	G28:43	Goshen	(413) 268-7098
Demarest Lloyd State Park	O33:50	Dartmouth	(508) 636-8816
Dighton Rock State Park	O31:50	Berkeley	(508) 822-7537 (508) 644-5522
Douglas State Forest	L30:49	Douglas	(508) 476-7872
Dubuque Memorial State Forest	G27:43	Hawley	(413) 339-5504
Dunn Pond State Park	K27:44	Gardner	(978) 632-7897
Ellisville Harbor State Park	Q31:51	Plymouth	(508) 866-2580
Erving State Forest	J27:43	Erving	(978) 544-3939
F Gilbert Hills State Forest	N30:50	Foxborough	(508) 543-5850
Fall River Heritage State Park	N32:50	Fall River	(508) 675-5759
Federated Womens Club State Forest	J28:43	Petersham	(978) 939-8962
Fort Phoenix State Reservation	P32:50	Fairhaven	(508) 992-4524
Franklin State Forest	M30:49	Franklin	
Freetown State Forest	O31:50	Assonet	(508) 644-5522
Gardner Heritage State Park	K27:44	Gardner	(978) 630-1497
Georgetown Rowley State Park	O27:45	Georgetown, Rowley	(978) 887-5931
Granville State Forest	F30:47	Granville	(413) 357-6611
Great Brook Farm State Park	N27:45	Carlisle	(978) 369-6312
Great Meadows National Wildlife Refuge	N28:45	Sudbury	(978) 443-4661
Halibut Point State Park	P27:45	Rockport	(978) 546-2997
Hampton Ponds State Park	H29:43	Westfield	(413) 532-3985
Harold Parker State Forest	O27:45	North Andover	(978) 686-3391
HO Cook State Forest	G26:43	Heath, Colrain	(413) 339-5504
Holland Pond State Park	K30:49	Holland	
Holyoke Heritage State Park	H29:43	Holyoke	(413) 534-1723
Holyoke Range State Park	H29:43	Amherst	(413) 586-0350
Hopkinton State Park	M29:44	Hopkinton	(508) 435-4303
Horseneck Beach State Forest	O33:50	Westport	(508) 636-8816
Hubbardston State Forest	K28:44	Hubbardston	
Lake Dennison State Park	K27:44	Winchendon	(978) 939-8962
Lawrence Heritage State Park	N27:45	Lawrence	(978) 791-1655
Leominster State Forest	L28:44	Westminster	(978) 874-2303
Lowell Dracut Tyngsborough State Forest	N27:45	Lowell, Dracut, Tyngsborough	(978) 453-0592
Lowell Heritage State Park	N27:45	Lowell	(978) 453-0592
Lynn Heritage State Park	O28:45	Lynn	(781) 598-1974
Manuel Corellus State Forest	Q33:51	Marthas Vineyard	(508) 693-2540
Massasoit State Park	O31:50	Taunton	(508) 822-7405
Maudslay State Park	O26:45	Newburyport	(978) 465-7223
Middlefield State Forest	F28:42	Middlefield	(413) 442-8992
Mohawk Trail State Forest	G27:43	Charlemont	(413) 339-5504
Monomoy National Wildlife Refuge	S32:51	Chatham	(508) 945-0594
Monroe State Forest	F26:42	Monroe	(413) 339-5504
Moore State Park	K29:44	Paxton	(508) 792-3969
Mt Everett State Reservation	E30:47	Mt Washington	(413) 528-0330
Mt Grace State Forest	J27:43	Warwick	(508) 544-3939
Mt Greylock State Reservation	F27:42	Lanesborough	(413) 449-4267
Mt Sugarloaf State Reservation	H28:43	Deerfield	(413) 545-5993
Mt Tom State Reservation	H29:43	Holyoke	(413) 527-4805
Mt Washington State Forest	E30:47	Mt Washington	(413) 528-0330
Myles Standish Monument State Reservation	P30:50	Duxbury	(508) 866-2580
Myles Standish State Forest	P31:50	Carver, Plymouth	(508) 866-2526
Nantucket National Wildlife Refuge	S33:51	Nantucket	(978) 443-4661
Nickerson State Park	S31:51	Brewster	(508) 896-3491
Northfield State Forest	J27:43	Northfield	(978) 544-3939
October Mountain State Forest	F28:42	Lee	(413) 243-1778
Otis State Forest	F29:42	Otis	
Otter River State Forest	K27:44	Baldwinville	(978) 939-8962
Oxbow National Wildlife Refuge	M28:44	Lancaster	(978) 443-4661
Parker River National Wildlife Refuge	P26:45	Newburyport	(978) 465-5753
Pearl Hill State Park	L27:44	West Townsend	(508) 597-8802
Peru State Forest	F28:42	Peru	(413) 442-8992
Petersham State Forest	J27:43	Petersham	
Pilgrim Memorial State Park	P30:50	Plymouth	(508) 866-2580
Pittsfield State Forest	E28:42	Pittsfield	(413) 442-8992
Purgatory Chasm State Reservation	L30:49	Sutton	(508-234-3733
Quinsigamond State Park	L29:44	Worcester	(508) 755-6880
Robinson State Park	H30:48	Agawam	(413) 786-2877
Roxbury Heritage State Park	O29:45	Roxbury	(617) 445-3399
Rutland State Park	K28:44	Rutland	(508) 886-6333
Salisbury Beach State Reservation	P26:45	Salisbury	(978) 462-4481
Sandisfield State Forest	F30:47	Sandisfield	(413) 229-8212 (413) 528-0904
Sandy Point State Reservation	P27:45	Ipswich	(978) 462-4481
Savoy Mountain State Forest	F27:42	Savoy	(413) 663-8469
Scusset Beach State Reservation	Q31:51	Sandwich	(508) 888-0859
Shawme Crowell State Forest	Q31:51	Sandwich	(508) 888-0351
Skinner State Park	H29:43	Hadley	(413) 586-0350
South Cape Beach State Park	Q32:51	Mashpee	(508) 457-0495
South River State Forest	H27:43	Conway	(413) 268-7098
Spencer State Forest	K29:44	Spencer	(508) 886-6333
Taconic Trail State Park	E26:42	Williamstown	(413) 499-4262
Templeton State Forest	K28:44	Templeton	
Tolland State Forest	F29:42	Otis	(413) 269-6002
Upton State Forest	M29:44	Upton	(508) 278-6436
Wachusett Mountain State Reservation	L28:44	Princeton	(978) 464-2987
Waconah Falls State Park	F28:42	Dalton	(413) 442-8992
Walden Pond State Reservation	N28:45	Concord	(978) 369-3254
Waquoit Bay Research Reserve	Q32:51	Mashpee	(508) 457-0495
Warwick State Forest	J27:43	Warwick	(978) 544-6536
Watson Pond State Park	O30:50	Taunton	
Webb Memorial State Park	O29:45	Weymouth	(781) 740-1605
Wells State Park	K29:44	Sturbridge	(508) 347-9257
Wendell State Forest	J27:43	Wendell	(413) 659-3797
Western Gateway Heritage State Park	F27:42	North Adams	(413) 663-6312
Whitehall State Park	M29:44	Hopkinton	(508) 435-4303
Willard Brook State Forest	L27:44	Ashby, Townsend	(978) 597-8802
Willowdale State Forest	O27:45	Ipswich	(978) 887-5931
Winchendon State Forest	K27:44	Winchendon	
Windsor State Forest	F27:42	Windsor	(413) 663-8469
Wompatuck State Park	P29:45	Hingham	(781) 749-7160
Wrentham State Forest	N30:50	Wrentham	

NEW HAMPSHIRE

Feature Name	Grid:Page	Community	Phone
Alton Bay State Forest	N22:39	Alton	(603) 796-2323
Annette State Forest	K26:44	Rindge, Sharon	(603) 271-3456
Annie Duncan State Forest	J22:37	Plainfield	(603) 796-2323
Ballard State Park	N26:45	Derry	(603) 271-3456
Bear Brook State Park	N24:39	Allenstown	(603) 485-9874
Bedell Bridge State Historic Site	K19:29	Haverhill	(603) 547-3373
Belknap Mountain State Forest	N22:39	Guilford	(603) 796-2323
Benton State Forest	L20:29	Benton	(603) 788-4157
Biney Pond State Forest	L26:44	New Ipswich	
Black Mountain State Forest	K19:29	Haverhill	(603) 788-4157
Blair State Forest	M21:29	Campton	(603) 796-2323
Blue Job State Forest	O23:39	Farmington	(603) 271-3456
Cardigan State Park	L21:29	Orange	(603) 547-3373
Casals State Forest	L26:44	Peterborough	(603) 271-3456
Chemung State Forest	M22:38	Meredith	(603) 796-2323
Chesterfield Gorge Natural Area	J25:37	Chesterfield	(603) 271-3456
Clough State Park	L24:38	Weare	(603) 529-7112
Coleman State Park	N15:20	Stewartstown	(603) 538-6965
Connecticut Lakes State Forest	N13:10	Pittsburg	(603) 788-4157
Connecticut River State Forest	J24:37	Charlestown	(603) 271-3456
Conway Commonlands	O19:30	Conway	(603) 788-4157
Crawford Notch State Park	M19:29	Harts Location	(603) 374-2272
Daniel Webster Historical Site	L23:38	Franklin	(603) 934-5057
Dixville Notch State Park	N15:20	Dixville	(603) 323-2087
Dodge Brook State Forest	J24:37	Lempster	(603) 271-3456
Echo Lake State Park	N19:30	Conway	(603) 356-2672
Ellacoya State RV Park	N22:39	Gilford	(603) 293-7821

Feature Name	Grid:Page	Community	Phone
Forest Lake State Park	L18:29	Dalton	(603) 788-4157
Fox Forest	L24:38	Hillsborough	(603) 271-3456
Franconia Notch State Park	L19:29	Franconia Notch	(603) 823-8800
George Duncan State Forest	L22:38	New Hampton	(603) 796-2323
Gile State Forest	K22:38	Grantham	(603) 796-2323
Greenfield State Park	L25:38	Greenfield	(603) 547-3497
Hampton State Beach	P26:39	Hampton	(603) 926-3784
Harriman-Chandler State Forest	L24:38	Warner	(603) 271-3456
Heath Pond Bog	O21:30	Effingham, Ossipee	(603) 796-2323
Hemenway State Forest	N20:30	Tamworth	(603) 796-2323
Honey Brook State Forest	J24:37	Marlow	(603) 271-3456
Hubbard Hill State Forest	J24:37	Charlestown	(603) 271-3456
Jenness State Beach	P26:39	Rye	(603) 436-9404
Kingston State Park	O25:39	Kingston	(603) 642-5471
Lake Francis State Park	N14:20	Pittsburg	(603) 538-6965
Leighton State Forest	K25:38	Dublin	(603) 271-3456
Litchfield State Forest	M26:44	Litchfield	(603) 271-3456
Livermore Falls State Forest	M21:29	Campton	(603) 796-2323
Low State Forest	K24:38	Bradford, Hillsborough	(603) 271-3456
Mascoma State Forest	K21:29	Canaan	(603) 796-2323
Mast Yard State Forest	L24:38	Hopkinton	(603) 271-3456
Merriam State Forest	O19:30	Bartlett	(603) 788-4157
Milan Hill State Park	N17:20	Milan	(603) 482-3373
Miller State Park	L26:44	Peterborough	(603) 924-3672
Mollidgewock State Park	N16:20	Errol	(603) 788-4157
Monadnock State Park	K26:44	Jaffrey	(603) 532-8862
Moose Brook State Park	N17:20	Gorham	(603) 466-3860
Mount Major State Forest	N22:39	Alton	(603) 796-2323
Mount Washington State Park	N18:30	Sargents Purchase	(603) 466-3347
Mt Sunapee State Park and Beach	K23:38	Newbury	(603) 763-5561
Nash Stream Forest	M16:19	Stark, Odell	(603) 788-4157
North Beach State Park	P26:39	Hampton	(603) 926-6705
Northwood Meadows State Park	N24:39	Northwood	(603) 271-3456
Odiorne Point State Park	P26:39	Rye	(603) 436-7406
Paugus Bay State Forest	M22:38	Laconia	(603) 796-2323
Pawtuckaway State Park	N24:39	Nottingham	(603) 895-3031
Pillsbury State Park	K24:38	Washington	(603) 863-2860
Pine River State Forest	O21:30	Effingham, Ossipee	(603) 796-2323
Pisgah State Park	H26:43	Chester/Hinsdale	(603) 239-8153
Prescott State Forest	M22:38	Laconia	(603) 796-2323
Province Road State Forest	K21:29	Dorchester, Groton	(603) 697-2323
Reeds Ferry State Forest	M25:38	Bedford	(603) 271-3456
Rhododendron State Park	J26:43	Fitzwilliam	(603) 532-8862
Robert Frost Farm	N26:45	Derry	(603) 432-3091
Rollins State Park	L23:38	Warner	(603) 456-3808
Russell Shears State Forest	M24:38	Concord	(603) 271-3456
Russell-Abbott State Forest	L26:44	Mason, Wilton	(603) 271-3456
Scribner-Fellows State Forest	M21:29	Center Harbor	(603) 796-2323
Sentinel Mountain State Forest	K20:29	Piermont	(603) 786-4157
Shaker State Forest	M23:38	Canterbury	(603) 796-2323
Shieling State Forest	K26:44	Peterborough	(603) 271-3457
Silver Lake State Park	M26:44	Peterborough	(603) 271-3456
Sky Pond State Forest	M21:29	Center Harbor	(603) 796-2323
Soucook River State Forest	M23:38	Loudon	
St Gaudens National Historic Site	J22:37	Cornish	(603) 675-2175
State Forest Nursery	L23:38	Franklin	(603) 796-2323
Swain State Forest	M22:38	Laconia	(603) 796-2323
Trotten Trails State Forest	L24:38	Henniker	
Umbagog State Park	O16:20	Errol	(603) 786-4157
Vincent State Forest	L24:38	Deering, Weare	(603) 271-3456
Wade State Forest	L22:38	Hill	(603) 796-2323
Wantastiquet Mountain Natural Area	H26:43	Chesterfield	(603) 271-3456
Weeks State Park	M17:19	Lancaster	(603) 786-4157
Wellington Beach State Park	L22:38	Bristol	(603) 744-2197
Welton Falls State Forest	L21:29	Alexandria	(603) 796-2323
Wentworth State Beach	O22:39	Wolfeboro	(603) 569-3699
White Lake State Park	N20:30	Tamworth	(603) 323-7350
Winslow State Park	L23:38	Wilmot	(603) 526-6168

RHODE ISLAND

Feature Name	Grid:Page	Community	Phone
Arcadia Management Area	L32:49	Hopkinton, Exeter	(401) 539-2356
Beavertail State Park	N33:50	Jamestown	(401) 423-9941
Big River Management Area	M32:49	West Greenwich	(401) 222-6800
Black Hut Management Area	M30:49	Burrillville	(401) 222-6800
Block Island National Wildlife Refuge	M34:55	New Shoreham	(401) 364-9124
Brenton Point State Park	N33:50	Newport	(401) 847-2400
Buck Hill Management Area	L30:49	Burrillville	(401) 222-6800
Burlingame Management Area	L33:49	Charlestown	(401) 222-6800
Burlingame State Park	L33:49	Charlestown	(401) 322-8910
Carolina Management Area	L33:49	Richmond	(401) 222-6800
Charlestown Breachway	M34:55	Charlestown	(401) 364-7000
Colt State Park	N32:50	Bristol	(401) 253-7482
Durfee Hill Management Area	L31:49	Glocester	(401) 222-6800
East Beach	L34:55	Charlestown	(401) 322-0450
East Matunuck State Beach	M33:49	South Kingstown	(401) 789-8585
Fisherman's Memorial State Park	M33:49	Narragansett	(401) 789-8374
Fort Adams State Park	N33:50	Newport	(401) 847-2400
Fort Wetherill State Park	N33:50	Jamestown	(401) 423-1771
Fred Benson Beach	M34:55	New Shoreham	(401) 466-2611
George Washington Memorial Management Area	L31:49	Burrillville	(401) 222-6800
Goddard Memorial State Park	M32:49	Warwick	(401) 884-2010
Great Swamp Management Area	M33:49	South Kingstown	(401) 222-6800
Haines Memorial State Park	N31:50	Barrington	(401) 253-7482
Lincoln Woods State Park	M31:49	Lincoln	(401) 723-7892
Misquamicut State Beach	L34:55	Westerly	(401) 596-9097
Nicholas Farm Management Area	L32:49	Coventry	(401) 222-6800
Ninigret National Wildlife Refuge	M33:49	Charlestown	(401) 364-9124
Roger Wheeler State Beach	M33:49	Narragansett	(401) 789-3563
Sachuest Point National Wildlife Refuge	N33:50	Middletown	(401) 847-5511
Scarborough North & South Beach	M33:49	Narragansett	(401) 789-2324 (401) 782-1319
Trustom Pond National Wildlife Refuge	M33:49	South Kingstown	(401) 364-9124
Wickaboxet Management Area	L32:49	West Greenwich	(401) 222-6800
World War II Memorial State Park	M30:49	Woonsocket	(401) 762-9717

VERMONT

Feature Name	Grid:Page	Community	Phone
Alburg Dunes State Park	E15:17	Alburg	(800) 252- 2363
Allis State Park	H19:28	Randolph	(802) 276-3175
Ascutney State Park	J23:37	Windsor	(802) 674-2060
Ball Mountain Lake Recreation Area	G24:37	Jamaica	(802) 874-4881
Big Branch Recreation Area	G23:37	Manchester Center	(802) 362-2307
Big Deer State Park	J18:28	Groton	(802) 584-3823
Boulder Beach State Park	J18:28	Groton	(802) 584-3824
Branbury State Park	F20:27	Brandon	(802) 247-5825
Brandon Brook Recreation Area	G20:28	Rochester	(802) 767-4261
Brighton State Park	L15:19	Island Pond	(802) 723-4360
Burton Island State Park	E15:17	St. Albans Bay	(802) 524-6353
Button Bay State Park	E19:27	Vergennes	(802) 475-2377
Calvin Coolidge State Park	H22:37	Bridgewater Corners	(802) 672-3612
Camel's Hump State Park	G18:28	Duxbury, Huntington, Bolton	(802) 879-6565
Camp Plymouth State Park	H22:37	Ludlow	(802) 228-2025
CCC's Camp	G20:28	Rochester	(802) 767-4261
Chittenden Brook Recreation Area	G20:28	Rochester	(802) 767-4261
Crystal Lake State Park	K15:19	Barton	(802) 525-6205
D.A.R. State Park	E19:27	Addison	(802) 759-2354
Dutton Pines State Park	H25:37	Dummerston	
Elmore State Park	H17:18	Elmore	(802) 888-2982
Emerald Lake State Park	F23:36	East Dorset	(802) 362-1655
Falls of Lana Recreation Area	F20:27	Middlebury	(802) 388-4362
Fort Dummer State Park	H26:43	Brattleboro	(802) 254-2610
Gifford Woods State Park	G21:28	Killington	(802) 775-5354
Grand Isle State Park	E16:17	Grand Isle	(802) 372-4300
Greendale Recreation Area	G23:37	Manchester Center	(802) 362-2307
Groton State Forest	J18:28	Groton	
Grout Pond Recreation Area	G25:37	Manchester Center	(802) 362-2307
Half Moon Pond State Park	F21:37	Hubbardton	(802) 273-2848
Hancock Overlook State Park	G20:28	Hancock	(802) 767-4261
Hapgood Recreation Area	G24:37	Manchester Center	(802) 362-2307
Jamaica State Park	G24:37	Jamaica	(802) 874-4600
Jay Peak State Forest	H15:18	Westfield	
Kettle Pond State Park	J18:28	Groton	(802) 584-3820
Kill Kare State Park	G14:18	St. Albans Bay	(802) 534-6021
Kingsland Bay State Park	E18:27	Ferrisburgh	(802) 877-3445
Knight Island State Park	E15:17	North Hero	(802) 524-6353
Knight Point State Park	E15:17	North Hero	(802) 372-8389
Lake Bomoseen State Park	F21:37	Fair Haven	(802) 265-4242
Lake Carmi State Park	G14:18	Enosburg Falls	(802) 933-8383
Lake Shaftsbury State Park	F25:36	Shaftsbury	(802) 375-9978
Lake St. Catherine State Park	F22:36	Poultney	(802) 287-9158
Little River State Park	G17:18	Waterbury	(802) 244-7103
Maidstone State Park	M16:19	North Strafford	(802) 676-3930
Molly Stark State Park	G26:43	Wilmington	(802) 464-5460
Moosalamo Recreation Area	F20:27	Middlebury	(802) 388-4362
Mount Mansfield State Forest	G17:18	Waterbury/ Stowe	
Mt. Philo State Park	F18:27	North Ferrisburgh	(802) 425-2390
New Discovery State Park	J18:28	Marshfield	(802) 584-3820
North Hartland Lake Recreation Area	J22:37	North Hartland	(802) 295-2855
North Hero State Park	E15:17	North Hero	(802) 372-8727
North Springfield Lake Recreation Area	H23:37	Springfield	(802) 886-2775
Peavine Recreation Area	G21:28	Stockbridge	(802) 767-4261
Quechee State Park	J22:37	White River Junction	(802) 295-2990
Red Mill State Park	F25:36	Manchester Center	(802) 362-2307
Ricker Pond State Park	J18:28	Groton	(802) 584-3821
Riverbend Recreation Area	G20:28	Rochester	(802) 767-4261
Robert Frost Wayside Area and Trail	F20:27	Middlebury	(802) 388-4362
Sand Bar State Park	F16:16	Milton	(802) 372-8240
Seyon Ranch State Park	J18:28	Groton	(802) 584-3829
Silver Lake State Park	H21:28	Barnard	(802) 234-9451
Smugglers' Notch State Park	G16:18	Stowe	(802) 253-4014
Stillwater Recreation Area	J18:28	Groton	(802) 584-3822
Stoughton Pond Recreation Area	H23:37	Perkinsville	(802) 886-2775
Texas Falls Recreation Area	G20:28	Rochester	(802) 767-4261
Thetford Hill State Park	J21:28	Thetford	(802) 785-2266
Townshend Lake Recreation Area	G25:37	Townshend	(802) 874-4881
Townshend State Park	G25:37	Newfane	(802) 365-7500
Underhill State Park	G17:18	Underhill	(802) 899-3022
Union Village Dam Recreation Area	J20:28	Union Village	(802) 295-2855
Waterbury Center State Park	G18:28	Waterbury	(802) 244-1266
White Rocks Recreation Area	G22:37	Manchester Center	(802) 362-2307
Wilgus State Park	J23:37	Ascutney	(802) 674-5422
Willoughby State Forest	K16:19	Sutton/ Westmore	
Winhall Brook Camping Area	G24:37	Londonderry	
Woodford State Park	F26:42	Woodford	(802) 447-7169
Wood's Island State Park	G14:18	St. Albans Bay	(802) 524-6353
Wrightsville Dam Recreation Area	H18:28	Middlesex	

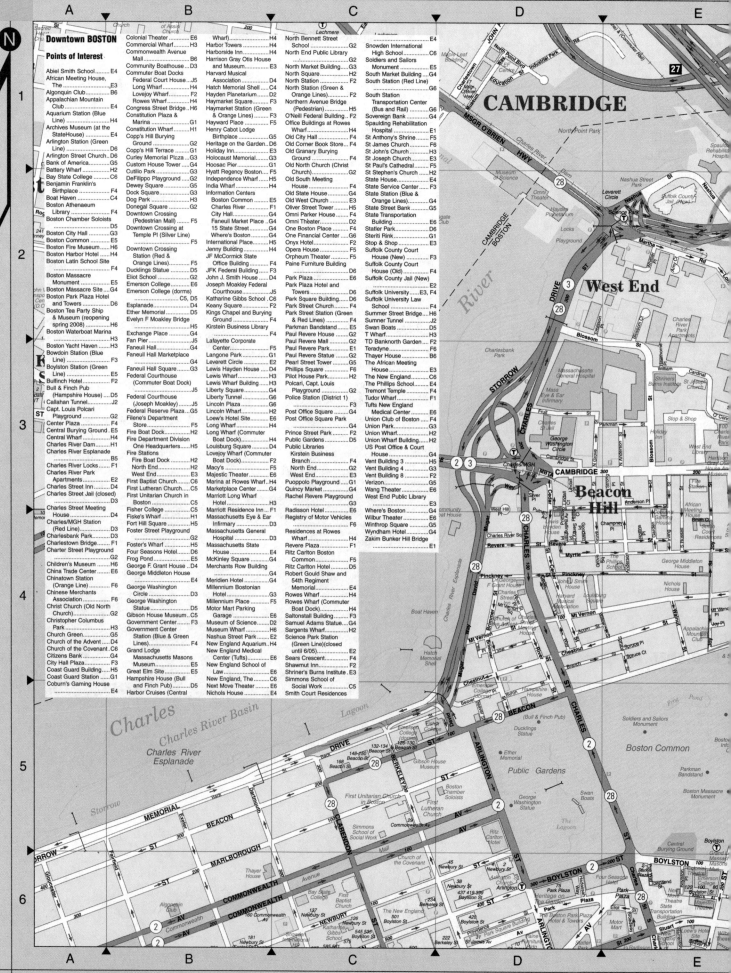

N

Downtown BOSTON

Points of Interest

Abiel Smith School........E4
African Meeting House,
  The E3
Algonquin Club...........B6
Appalachian Mountain
  Club C5
Aquarium Station (Blue
  Line) E4
Archives Museum (at the
  StateHouse).............F4
Arlington Station (Green
  Line) D6
Arlington Street Church..G5
Bank of America..........G5
Battery Wharf............H2
Bay State College........C6
Benjamin Franklin's
  Birthplace F5
Boat Haven...............C4
Boston Athenaeum
  Library F4
Boston Chamber Soloists
  ....D5
Boston City Hall.........G3
Boston Common............E5
Boston Fire Museum.......H6
Boston Harbor Hotel......H4
Boston Latin School Site
Boston Massacre
  Monument E5
Boston Massacre Site.....G4
Boston Park Plaza Hotel
  and Towers..............D6
Boston Tea Party Ship
  & Museum (reopening
  spring 2008).............H6
Boston Waterboat Marina
  ....H3
Boston Yacht Haven.......H3
Bowdoin Station (Blue
  Line) F3
Boylston Station (Green
  Line) E5
Bulfinch Hotel...........F2
Bull & Finch Pub
  (Hampshire House) D5
Callahan Tunnel..........J2
Capt. Louis Polcari
  Playground G2
Center Plaza.............F4
Central Burying Ground ..E5
Central Wharf............H4
Charles River Dam........H1
Charles River Esplanade
  ....B5
Charles River Locks......F1
Charles River Park
  Apartments E2
Charles Street Inn.......D4
Charles Street Jail (closed)
  ....D3
Charles Street Meeting
  House D4
Charles/MGH Station
  (Red Line)..............D3
Charlesbank Park.........D3
Charlestown Bridge.......F1
Charter Street Playground
  ....G2
Children's Museum H6
China Trade Center E6
Chinatown Station
  (Orange Line) F6
Chinese Merchants
  Association F6
Christ Church (Old North
  Church)................D4
Christopher Columbus
  Park H3
Church Dam...............H3
Church of the Advent D4
Church of the Covenant ..C6
Citizens Bank G4
City Hall Plaza..........F3
Coast Guard Building.....H5
Coast Guard Station G1
Coburn's Gaming House
  ....E4

Colonial Theater E6
Commercial Wharf.........H3
Commonwealth Avenue
  Mall B6
Community Boathouse......D3
Commuter Boat Docks
  Federal Court House.....H4
  Long Wharf..............H4
  Lovejoy Wharf..........F2
  Rowes Wharf.............H4
Congress Street Bridge...H6
Constitution Plaza &
  Marina G1
Constitution Wharf.......H1
Copp's Hill Burying
  Ground G2
Copp's Hill Terrace G2
Curley Memorial Plaza....G3
Custom House Tower G4
Cutillo Park G3
DeFilippo Playground G2
Dewey Square.............G5
Dock Square..............G4
Dog Park H3
Donegal Square...........G2
Downtown Crossing
  (Pedestrian Mall) F5
Downtown Crossing at
  Temple Pl (Silver Line) .F5
Downtown Crossing
  Station (Red &
  Orange Lines)...........F5
Ducklings Statue D5
Eliot School G2
Emerson College..........E6
Emerson College (dorms)
  ....C5, D4
Esplanade D4
Ether Memorial D5
Evelyn F Moakley Bridge
  ....H5
Exchange Place...........G4
Fan Pier J5
Faneuil Hall.............G4
Faneuil Hall Marketplace
  ....G4
Faneuil Hall Square......G3
Federal Courthouse
  (Commuter Boat Dock)
  ....J5
Federal Reserve Plaza....G5
Federal Courthouse
  (Joseph Moakley).......J5
Filene's Department
  Store F5
Fire Boat Dock...........H2
Fire Department Division
  One Headquarters........H5
Fire Stations
  Fire Boat Dock..........H2
  North End...............H2
  West End................E3
First Baptist Church.....C6
First Lutheran Church....C5
First Unitarian Church in
  Boston C5
Fisher College C5
Fiske's Wharf............H1
Fort Hill Square.........H5
Foster Street Playground
  ....G2
Foster's Wharf...........H5
Four Seasons Hotel.......D6
Frog Pond E5
George F. Grant House ...D4
George Middleton House
  ....E4
George Washington
  Circle D3
George Washington
  Statue C5
Gibson House Museum......C5
Government Center F3
Government Center
  Station (Blue & Green
  Lines)..................F4
Grand Lodge
  Massachusetts Masons
  Museum..................F4
Great Elm Site...........E5
Hampshire House (Bull
  and Finch Pub)..........D5
Harbor Cruises (Central

Wharf)...................H4
Harbor Towers...........H4
Harborside Inn...........H4
Harrison Gray Otis House
  and Museum..............E3
Harvard Musical
  Association D4
Hatch Memorial Shell.....C4
Hayden Planetarium.......D2
Haymarket Square.........F3
Haymarket Station (Green
  & Orange Lines).........F3
Hayward Place............F5
Henry Cabot Lodge
  Birthplace..............F4
Heritage on the Garden..D6
Holiday Inn..............E3
Holocaust Memorial.......G3
Hoosac Pier..............G1
Hyatt Regency Boston.....F5
Independence Wharf.......H5
India Wharf..............H4
Information Centers
  Boston Common...........E5
  Charles River F1
  City Hall...............F4
  Faneuil Market Place ...G4
  15 State Street.........G4
  Where's Boston G4
International Place.......H5
Jenny Building G4
JF McCormick State
  Office Building.........F4
JFK Federal Building.....F3
John J. Smith House D4
Joseph Moakley Federal
  Courthouse..............J5
Katharine Gibbs School .C6
Keany Square.............F2
Kings Chapel and Burying
  Ground F4
Kirstein Business Library
Lafayette Corporate
  Center..................F5
Langone Park.............G1
Leverett Circle E2
Lewis Hayden House D4
Lewis Wharf H3
Lewis Wharf Building.....H3
Liberty Square...........G4
Liberty Tunnel G6
Lincoln Plaza F6
Lincoln Wharf...........H2
Loew's Hotel Site........F6
Long Wharf H4
Long Wharf (Commuter
  Boat Dock)..............H4
Louisburg Square D4
Lovejoy Wharf (Commuter
  Boat Dock)..............F2
Macy's F5
Majestic Theater E6
Marina at Rowes Wharf...H4
Marketplace Center G4
Marriott Long Wharf
  Hotel H3
Marriott Residence Inn ..F1
Massachusetts Eye & Ear
  Infirmary D3
Massachusetts General
  Hospital D3
Massachusetts State
  House E4
McKinley Square H4
Meridian Row Building
  Row Building F6
Meridian Hotel H4
Millennium Bostonian
  Hotel G3
Millennium Place F5
Motor Mart Parking
  Garage E6
Museum of Science........D2
Museum Wharf............H6
Nashua Street Park E2
New England Aquarium.....H4
New England Medical
  Center (Tufts)..........E6
New England School of
  Law E6
New England, The C6
Next Move Theater E6
Nichols House E4

North Bennett Street
  School G2
North End Public Library ..G2
North Market Building....G3
North Square G3
North Station F2
North Station (Green &
  Orange Lines)...........F2
Northern Avenue Bridge
  (Pedestrian)............H5
O'Neill Federal Building .F3
Office Buildings at Rowes
  Wharf...................H4
Old City Hall............F4
Old Corner Book Store....F4
Old Granary Burying
  Ground F4
Old North Church (Christ
  Church)................G2
Old South Meeting
  House F4
Old State House G4
Old West Church E3
Oliver Street Tower......H5
Omni Parker House F4
Omni Theater............D2
One Boston Place G4
One Financial Center G6
Onyx Hotel F2
Opera House F5
Orpheum Theater F5
Paine Furniture Building
  ....D6
Park Plaza Hotel and
  Towers D6
Park Square Building.....D6
Park Street Church F4
Park Street Station (Green
  & Red Lines)............F4
Parkman Bandstand E5
Paul Revere House G2
Paul Revere Mall G2
Paul Revere Square E1
Paul Revere Statue G2
Pearl Street Tower G5
Phillips Square F4
Pilot House Park.........H2
Polcari, Capt. Louis
  Playground G2
Police Station (District 1)
Post Office Square G4
Post Office Square Park
Prince Street Park G2
Public Libraries
  Kirstein Business
    Branch F4
  North End...............G2
  West End................E3
Puoppolo Playground G1
Quincy Market G4
Rachel Revere Playground
  ....G3
Radisson Hotel E6
Registry of Motor Vehicles
  ....F6
Residences at Rowes
  Wharf...................H4
Revere Plaza F1
Ritz Carlton Boston
  Common.................F5
Ritz Carlton Hotel D5
Robert Gould Shaw and
  54th Regiment
  Memorial E4
Rowes Wharf H4
Rowes Wharf (Commuter
  Boat Dock)..............H4
Saltonstall Building F3
Samuel Adams Statue......G4
Sargents Wharf...........H2
Science Park Station
  (Green Line)(closed
  until 6/05)..............E2
Sears Crescent F4
Shawmut Inn..............H4
Shriner's Burns Institute .E3
Simmons School of
  Social Work.............C5
Smith Court Residences

Snowden International
  High School.............C6
Soldiers and Sailors
  Monument E5
South Market Building....G4
South Station (Red Line) .G6
South Station
  Transportation Center
  (Bus and Rail)..........G6
Sovereign Bank G4
Spaulding Rehabilitation
  Hospital E1
St Anthony's Shrine F5
St James Church..........F6
St John's Church.........H3
St Joseph Church.........D4
St Paul's Cathedral......F5
St Stephen's Church G2
State House..............E4
State Service Center F3
State Station (Blue &
  Orange Lines)...........G4
State Street Bank........G5
State Transportation
  Building................E6
Statler Park.............D6
Steriti Rink G1
Stop & Shop E3
Suffolk County Court
  House (New) F3
Suffolk County Court
  House (Old) E2
Suffolk County Jail (New)
Suffolk University........E3, F4
Suffolk University Law
  School F4
Summer Street Bridge.....H6
Sumner Tunnel J2
Swan Boats D5
T Wharf H3
TD Banknorth Garden F2
Teradyne F6
Thayer House B6
The African Meeting
  House E4
The New England C6
The Phillips School E4
Tremont Temple F4
Tudor Wharf F1
Tufts New England
  Medical Center..........E6
Union Club of Boston E4
Union Park...............G3
Union Park...............G3
Union Wharf Building.....H2
US Post Office & Court
  House G4
Vent Building 3..........H5
Vent Building 4..........G3
Vent Building 8..........G3
Verizon F4
Wang Theater E6
West End Public Library
Where's Boston G4
Wilbur Theater E6
Winthrop Square G4
Wyndham Hotel G4
Zakim Bunker Hill Bridge
  ....E1

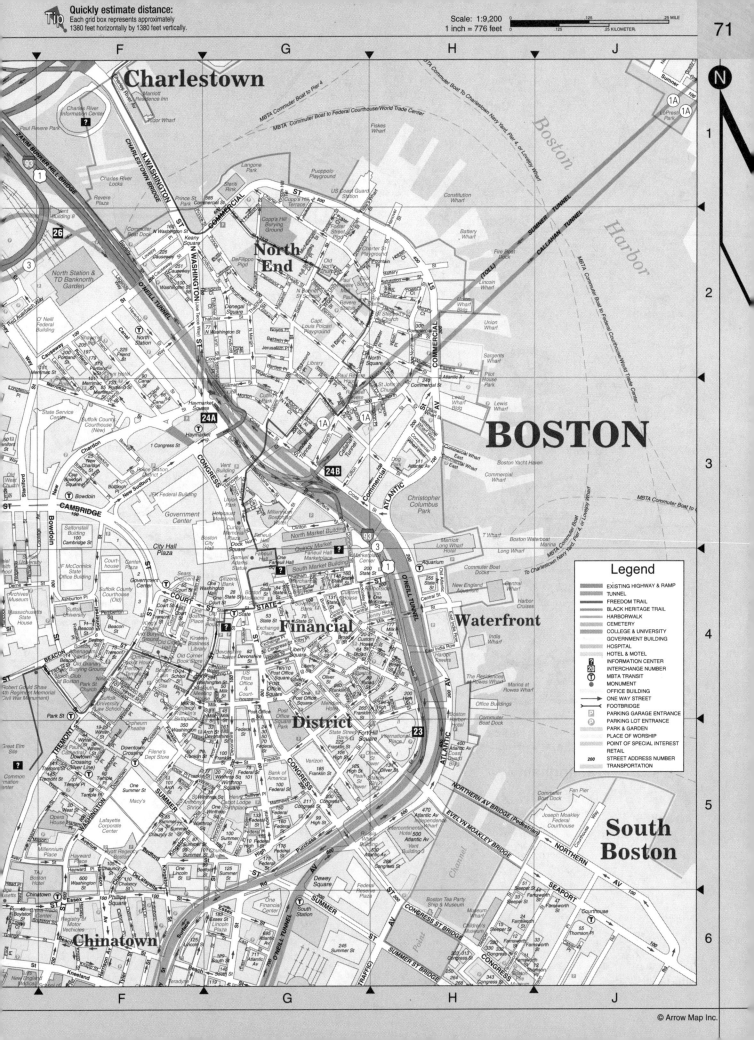

Massachusetts
Bay

BOSTON

Boston
Harbor

Logan
INTERNATIONAL
AIRPORT

Wakefield

Peabody

Marblehead

Salem

Stoneham

Lynn

Saugus

Swampscott

Melrose

Malden

Nahant

Revere

Everett

Chelsea

Winthrop

Cambridge

South
Boston

Roxbury

Quincy
Bay

North
Quincy

Milton

Quincy

Hull

Hingham
Bay

Hingham

Cohasset

Braintree

Weymouth

© Arrow Map Inc.

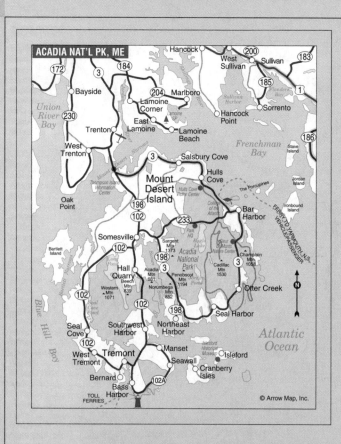

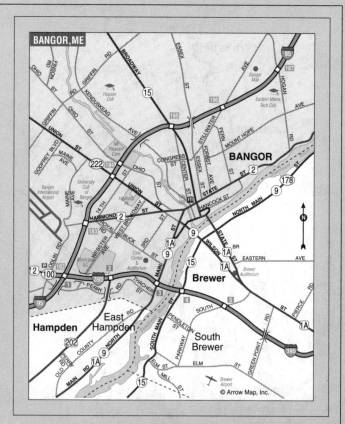

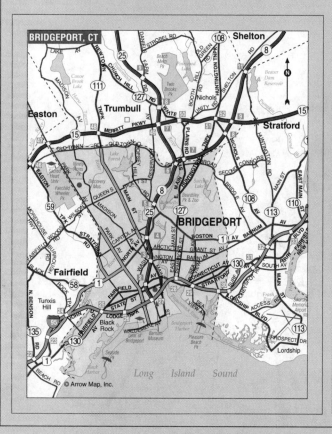

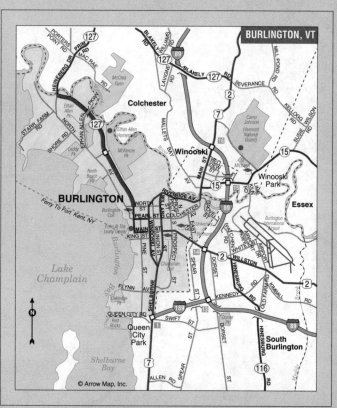

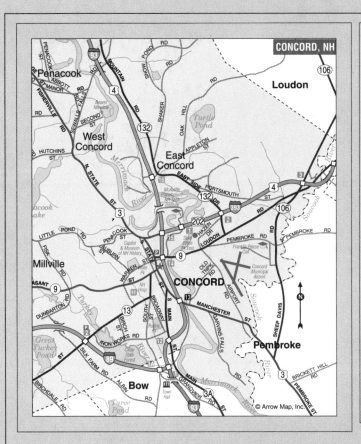

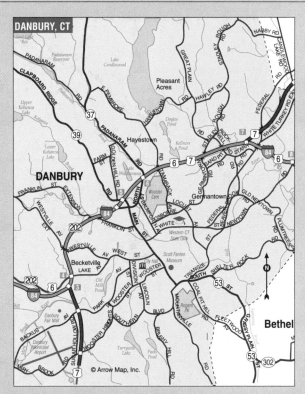

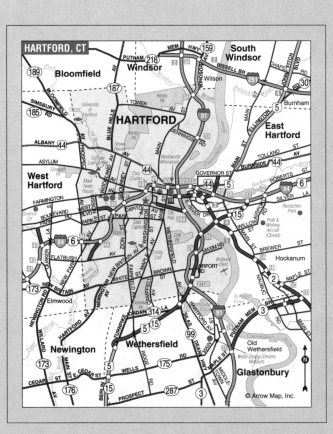

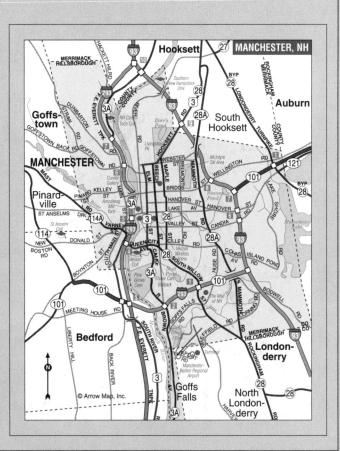

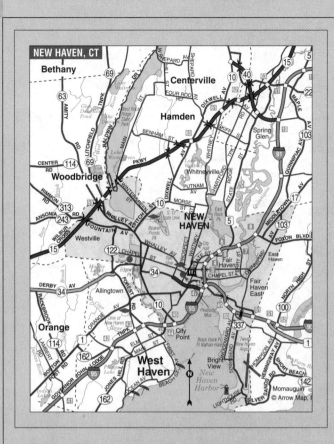

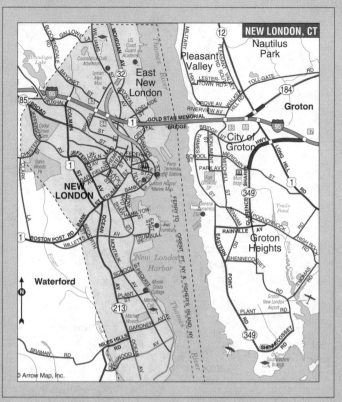

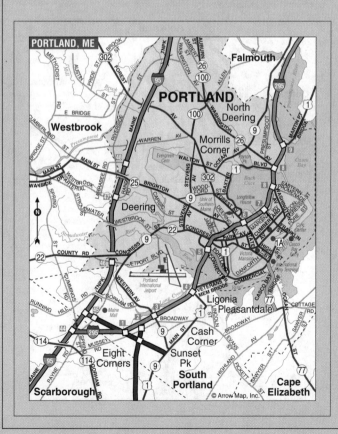

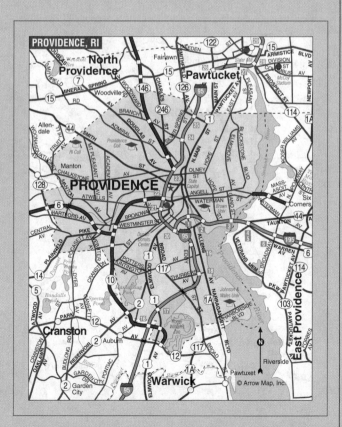

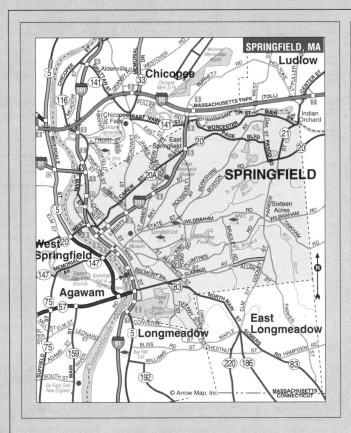

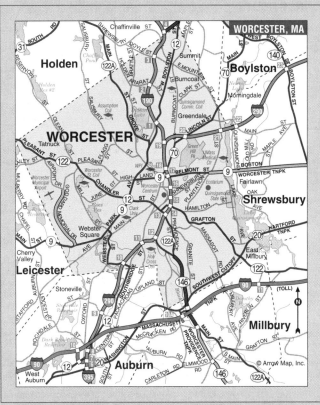

Special Points of Interest

CONNECTICUT

AMERICAN CLOCK AND WATCH MUSEUM (Grid F32:47) The museum traces the history of clock making in America, with 3,000 timepieces located in an historic 1801 house. (860) 583-6070.

BEARDSLEY ZOO (Grid F34:53) The zoo's 36 acres are devoted to the wildlife of North and South America, and also includes a farmyard, a picnic grove, and a carousel. (203) 394-6565.

DINOSAUR STATE PARK (Grid H32:48) Jurassic-period dinosaur tracks are enclosed within a geodesic dome. An 80-foot diorama depicts the setting in which the tracks were made. (860) 529-8423.

GILLETTE CASTLE (Grid H33:54) Perched high above the Connecticut River is the home of William Gillette, an actor made famous by his portrayal of Sherlock Holmes. Theatrically designed by Gillette, the castle features intricate woodwork and ingenious built-in furnishings. (860) 526-2336.

MARK TWAIN HOUSE (Grid G30:48) This fascinating 19-room Victorian Gothic mansion resembling a steamboat, with interiors designed by Louis Comfort Tiffany, was the author's home between 1874 and 1891. Guided tours are available. (860) 247-0998.

MYSTIC MARITIME AQUARIUM (Grid K34:55) The aquarium houses more than 3,500 living sea creatures, including sea lions, penguins, dolphins, and whales. (203) 572-5955.

MYSTIC SEAPORT (Grid K34:55) Board historic ships, visit period homes, and watch working craftspeople in this re-created whaling village, which is the world's largest maritime museum. Check out the only remaining 19th-Century whaler, the Charles W. Morgan, as well as the square-rigger Joseph Conrad, and the fishing schooner L.A. Dunton. (860) 572-5315.

NATHAN HALE HOMESTEAD (Grid J31:49) The family home of Connecticut's state hero is filled with original furnishings and family memorabilia. The house and surrounding farm reflects the lifestyle of the first generation of American citizens. (860) 742-6917.

NEW ENGLAND AIR MUSEUM (Grid H30:48) The largest aviation museum in the northeast has more than 80 historic aircraft, and many fascinating exhibits and films. (860) 623-3305.

OLD NEWGATE PRISON AND COPPER MINE (Grid G30:48) Tour America's first chartered copper mine, which later became Connecticut's first state prison. Hiking trails and a spectacular view add an extra plus to this site. (860) 653-3563.

PRUDENCE CRANDALL MUSEUM (Grid K32:49) New England's first school for Black women was founded in 1833 by Prudence Crandall, Connecticut's official state heroine. The museum contains period furnishings, changing exhibits, a research library and a gift shop. (860) 546-9916.

STATE CAPITOL (See Hartford Insert) Made of white Connecticut marble, this impressive building is adorned with gothic spires, a gold-leaf dome, and statues and medallions commemorating persons and events in state history. (860) 240-0222.

USS NAUTILUS AND SUBMARINE FORCE MUSEUM (Grid K33:49) Board the USS Nautilus, the world's first nuclear-powered submarine. The museum recounts the history of the U.S. Submarine Force. (860) 694-3174.

VALLEY RAILROAD STEAM TRAIN AND RIVERBOAT (Grid H34:54) Ride a steam train with restored coaches and take a return trip on a steamboat for a unique perspective of the scenic lower Connecticut River valley. (860) 767-0103.

WADSWORTH ATHENAEUM (See Hartford Insert) The nation's oldest public art museum was founded 1842. It houses nearly 50,000 works, including Hudson River School landscapes, 20th-Century figuratives, as well as abstract and pop art. (860) 278-2670.

YALE UNIVERSITY ART GALLERY (See New Haven Insert) This world-class museum on the Yale campus houses Asian, Gothic, and Renaissance collections, along with French Impressionists, and both 20th-Century American and European Modernists. (203) 432-0600.

MAINE

ACADIA NATIONAL PARK (Grid Z18:34) Spectacular ocean and mountain scenery on Mt Desert Island make Acadia one of the most popular National Parks. Scenic roads wind throughout the park, including the summit of Cadillac Mountain, the highest point (1,530 ft) on the Atlantic Coast. (207) 288-3338.

BAXTER STATE PARK (Grid W9:8) The park protects the natural beauty of its mountains and streams, and is dominated by Mt Katahdin, Maine's highest peak. (207) 723-5140.

BOOTHBAY RAILWAY VILLAGE (Grid U20:32) A recreated historical village that offers a narrow-gauge steam train ride as well as an exceptional antique automobile exhibit. (207) 633-4727.

BRICK STORE MUSEUM (Grid Q23:40) The Brick Store Museum is the center of Kennebunk's history, and the starting point for guided walking tours of Kennebunk's National Register Historic District. The complex includes the original 1825 brick store, and a Greek Revival house complete with barn and carriage stalls. (207) 985-4802.

DESERT OF MAINE (Grid R20:31) This 40-acre natural phenomenon occurred when severe erosion at an abandoned farm exposed a deposit of sand left by glaciers 10,000 years ago. Narrated tram tours and nature trails are available. The site includes a 1783 barn with a farm museum and the world's only Sand Museum. Children can also search for gemstones. (207) 865-6962.

EAGLE ISLAND (Grid S21:31) Summer home of North Pole explorer, Admiral Robert Peary. The island is accessible by boat during the summer, and offers house tours, as well as a hiking trail and picnic area. (207) 624-6080.

MAINE MARITIME MUSEUM (Grid T20:32) Located in the shipbuilding city of Bath, the museum preserves and interprets the maritime history of Maine through historical displays, boat building exhibits, vessel tours and multimedia galleries. (207) 443-1316.

MAINE WILDLIFE PARK (Grid Q20:31) The Maine Department of Inland Fisheries cares for injured and orphaned wildlife here in hopes of returning them to the wild. The 200-acre park often has moose, black bear, lynx, mountain lions, wild turkeys, bald eagles, and owls. (207) 657-4977.

OLD FORT WESTERN (Grid T18:32) Built in 1754, this is America's oldest surviving wooden fort. (207) 626-2385.

OWLS HEAD TRANSPORTATION MUSEUM (Grid W19:33) This museum has an impressive collection of pioneer aircraft, vintage cars, motorcycles, bicycles, carriages, and engines. (207) 594-4418.

ROOSEVELT CAMPOBELLO INTERNATIONAL PARK (Grid EE15:25) This international memorial to Franklin D. Roosevelt is located at his summer home. The park offers scenic vistas, picnic and observation areas, walking trails and beaches in a 2800-acre area. (506) 752-2922.

SABBATHDAY LAKE SHAKER COMMUNITY AND MUSEUM (Grid R20:31) Established in 1794, Sabbathday Lake is the only remaining active Shaker community, consisting of 18 well-maintained buildings. The site features a museum, store, library, guided tours and special programs. (207) 926-4597.

SARAH ORNE JEWETT HOUSE (Grid P24:39) One of the country's most celebrated regional writers, Jewett spent much of her life in this stately 1774 Georgian-style residence. (207) 384-2454.

SEASHORE TROLLEY MUSEUM (Grid Q23:41) This museum houses one of the world's oldest and largest collections of trolleys, including the New Orleans "Streetcar Named Desire." (207) 967-2712.

SS KATAHDIN AND MOOSEHEAD MARINE MUSEUM (Grid T12:12) The SS Katahdin is the centerpiece of the museum celebrating the history of steamboating on Moosehead Lake. Built in 1914, and later converted to diesel, the Katahdin was used as a towboat to haul booms of logs. Three-hour to all-day cruises are available. (207) 695-2716.

STATE HOUSE (Grid T18:32) An impressive building designed by Charles Bulfinch, and built between 1829-32. The dome rises 185 feet. (207) 287-1400.

WILLOWBROOK MUSEUM AT NEWFIELD (Grid P21:30) The largest 19th-Century village in New England, containing 37 buildings, 10,000 artifacts, over 65 carriages and sleighs, a carousel and a stage coach. (207) 793-2784.

MASSACHUSETTS

ARMORY NATIONAL HISTORIC SITE (Grid H30:48) In 1794, the first National Armory was established in Springfield. The museum maintains one of the world's most extensive and unique firearms collection. (413) 734-8551.

ARROWHEAD (Grid E28:42) The home of Herman Melville from 1850-1862, during the period he wrote Moby Dick, Arrowhead is a house museum interpreting the life of the Melville family in the Berkshires. (413) 442-1793.

BASKETBALL HALL OF FAME (Grid H30:48) Located in Springfield, the birthplace of basketball, this international shrine is comprised of ingenious exhibits honoring the game's great players, teams, and coaches. Also on display are TV clips, and photos of special events that have taken place since the inception of the sport in 1891. (413) 781-6500.

BOSTON COMMON (See Downtown Boston Insert) The country's oldest public park, and starting point for the Freedom Trail, this 44-acre park was originally used for the feeding of cattle and the training of militia.

BRIDGE OF FLOWERS (Grid G27:43) In 1929, a trolley bridge over the Deerfield River in Shelburne was transformed into a meticulously tended, 400-foot linear garden. Over 500 varieties of plantings assure beautiful flowers from April tulips to October chrysanthemums. (413) 625-2526.

CAPE COD NATIONAL SEASHORE (Grid S30:51) Forty miles of dramatic sand dunes and eroding cliffs, sea birds and gorgeous scenery, as well as bike and nature trails. Visitor Centers are located in Eastham and Provincetown. (508) 349-3785.

CHESTERWOOD (Grid E29:42) The 1920's home of sculptor Daniel Chester French, best known for the statue in the Lincoln Memorial, this tranquil 122-acre estate in Stockbridge offers a variety of exhibitions and events. (413) 298-3579.

CRANES BEACH AND CASTLE (Grid P27:45) Built in 1927, this 59-room Stuart mansion overlooks Cranes Beach. Tours, cultural events and corporate functions are held here. (978) 356-4351.

CRANE MUSEUM (Grid F28:42) Crane and Company, the major industry in Dalton, has produced all the paper that US currency is printed on since 1879. Housed in part of Zenas Crane's 1846 stone mill, the museum traces the history of papermaking starting from 1801. (413) 684-6481.

DICKINSON HOMESTEAD (Grid H28:43) Emily Dickinson, one of America's most beloved poets, lived all but 15 years of her life here at the family homestead in Amherst with its lovely grounds and garden. Open for public tours from March through mid-December. (413) 542-8161.

ECOTARIUM (See Worcester Insert) This 60-acre facility dedicated to environmental exploration offers a three-story museum, and features 60 species of wildlife ranging from polar bears to bald eagles, a unique tree canopy walkway, and a narrow-gauge railroad. (508) 929-2700.

FALL RIVER HERITAGE STATE PARK (Grid N32:50) Overlooking Battleship Cove, home of the WWII battleship USS Massachusetts, the park features an antique carousel, and public sailing programs. The Visitors Center tells the story of Fall River, the city that once produced more cotton textiles than any other in the Western Hemisphere. (508) 675-5759.

HAMMOND CASTLE MUSEUM (Grid P27:45) John Hays Hammond, a famous inventor known as "The Father of Remote Control," built this medieval-style castle in the 1920's to serve as his residence as well as his research lab, and as backdrop for his collection of Roman, Medieval and Renaissance artifacts, in addition to an 8,200-pipe organ. (978) 283-7673.

HANCOCK SHAKER VILLAGE (Grid E28:42) A 1200-acre open-air museum depicting the lifestyle of the Shakers, who lived here between 1781-1960. The site includes an unusual round stone barn, farm animals, craft demonstrations, Shaker furniture, and other original artifacts. (800) 817-1137.

HERITAGE PLANTATION OF SANDWICH (Grid Q31:51) Best when the rhododendrons are in bloom, this 76-acre showcase for the varied collections of J.K. Lily features military miniatures, antique firearms, a working 1912 carousel, three galleries of American art, and 37 antique cars, including Gary Cooper's 1930 Duesenberg. (508) 888-3300.

HISTORIC DEERFIELD (Grid H27:43) A National Historic Landmark, Deerfield is a collection of 14 18th and 19th-Century houses and the objects in them, as well as 1000 acres of surrounding farmland, making it one of New England's most beautiful and unspoiled villages. The Flynt Center of Early New England life is filled with some of the great decorative art treasures of the period. (413) 774-5581.

JOHN F. KENNEDY LIBRARY AND MUSEUM (Grid F10, Boston) Dramatically located at Columbia Point, this museum brings the Kennedy presidency to vivid life through films and exhibits. (617) 514-1600.

LOWELL HERITAGE STATE PARK (Grid N27:43) Lowell boasts a remarkable network of canals created to power the bustling textile mills along the water's edge. Today, visitors can enjoy canal rides, and explore exhibits showcasing Lowell's role in America's industrial history. (978) 369--6312.

MASSACHUSETTS STATE HOUSE (Grid E4:71) Located on historic Beacon Hill, the original brick front section with its gilded dome was designed by Charles Bulfinch, and built in 1798. The State House displays statues, paintings, battle flags and war relics. Guided tours are available. Across the street is the Col. Robert Gould Shaw Memorial by Augustus Saint-Gaudens, a tribute to the first black regiment to serve in the Civil War. (617) 727-3676.

MINUTEMAN NATIONAL HISTORICAL PARK (Grid N28:45) This 850-acre park preserves and interprets landscapes, sites and structures associated with the battles of Lexington and Concord. It includes the reconstructed North Bridge and Daniel Chester French's Minuteman statue, as well as The Wayside, home at various times of authors Louisa May Alcott, Nathaniel Hawthorne and Margaret Sidney. The Minuteman Visitors Center offers a 40-foot battle mural and a multimedia theater presentation about the events of April 18-19, 1775. (978) 369-6993.

MUSEUM OF SCIENCE (Grid D2:71) Located in Science Park on the Charles River, the museum has more than 450 interactive exhibits on natural history, physical science, medicine, and astronomy. The Mugar Omni Theatre and Hayden Planetarium have changing shows. (617) 723-2500.

MUSEUM WHARF (Grid H6:71) The Children's Museum offers four floors of hands-on exhibits for kids and adults, (Reopening April 2007) (617) 426-8855.

NANTUCKET WHALING MUSEUM (Grid S34:57) This museum houses an outstanding collection of whaling memorabilia, including a 40-foot finback skeleton, a world-renowned collection of scrimshaw, as well as portraits and paintings reflecting the history of whaling. (508) 228-1894.

NEW BEDFORD WHALING MUSEUM (Grid O32:50) Located in the restored 19th-Century waterfront of New England's preeminent whaling port, the Whaling Museum exhibits the complete skeleton of a blue whale, and the Lagoda, the world's largest ship model. Across the street is Seamen's Bethel, the distinctive "Whalemen's Chapel" described in Moby Dick. (508) 997-0046.

NEW ENGLAND AQUARIUM (Grid H4:71) Home to more than 12,000 aquatic animals, a giant ocean tank, exotic tropical fish, sharks, penguins, and turtles, the aquarium also offers sea lion and dolphin shows as well as whale-watching excursions. (617) 973-5200.

NORMAN ROCKWELL MUSEUM (Grid E29:42) More than 500 of the artist's original paintings and drawings, including many Saturday Evening Post and McCall's magazine covers, are on display in a 19th-Century Gothic Revival mansion. Also on exhibit are thousands of photos, models and scenes used by the artist. (413) 298-4100.

OLD STURBRIDGE VILLAGE (Grid K30:49) In this recreated 1830's village covering 200 acres, more than 40 period exhibits are staffed by costumed "citizens" presenting various aspects of New England life. Craft demonstrations are featured, along with restored houses, gardens, a school, a blacksmith shop, and a working farm. (800) SEE-1830.

PLIMOTH PLANTATION (Grid Q31:51) Costumed interpreters portray original colonists involved in the daily activities of 17th-Century life. Also see Mayflower II, a reproduction of the ship that brought the Pilgrims to America; and Hobbamock's Homesite, which recreates Native culture. (508) 746-1622.

PUBLIC GARDEN (Grid D5:70) America's first public botanical garden is located across Charles Street from the Common. The famous Swan Boats and an equestrian statue of George Washington are among its most popular features. (617) 635-4505.

SAUGUS IRONWORKS (Grid O28:45) Site of the first integrated ironworks in North America from 1646-1668, this open air museum features a reconstructed blast furnace, forge, rolling mill, working water wheels, and a 17th-Century house. (781) 233-0050.

SIX FLAGS OVER NEW ENGLAND (Grid H30:48) Located in Agawam, New England's largest family theme and water park offers an exiting mix of thrilling rides, crowd-pleasing shows and attractions including Warner Brothers cartoon characters. (413) 786-9300 x0.

TANGLEWOOD (Grid E28:42) Enjoy legendary music under the stars at the summer home of the Boston Symphony Orchestra. (617) 266-1492.

YANKEE CANDLE (Grid H28:43) The flagship store of the Yankee Candle Company in South Deerfield is also a major tourist attraction offering fun for the whole family. The complex offers hands-on demonstrations of candle making and a year-round Bavarian Christmas shopping village. (413) 665-5089.

NEW HAMPSHIRE

CANOBIE LAKE PARK (Grid N26:45) One of the finest traditional amusement parks in the country features the Yankee Cannonball roller coaster, Canobie Corkscrew, along with many other thrills, rides, and shows. Other activities and features include a lake cruise, flower gardens, and tree-lined promenades. (603) 893-3506.

CANTERBURY SHAKER VILLAGE (Grid M23:38) At its peak in 1850, 300 people lived, worked and worshiped in 100 buildings on 4,000 acres. Today, 24 original buildings on 694 acres are staffed by experts on Shaker history who help illustrate their way of life. Skilled craftsmen recreate traditional furniture and implements. A restaurant serves meals from traditional recipes. (603) 783-9511, (800) 982-9511.

CASTLE IN THE CLOUDS (Grid N21:30) This 1910 stone mansion was built by millionaire Thomas Plant on 5,200 acres of mountainside. Tours (including Castle Springs Water plant) are offered, as well as hiking and horseback riding. (603) 476-5900, (800) 729-2468.

CHRISTA MCAULIFFE PLANETARIUM (Grid M24:38) This building is a memorial to Concord High School's most famous teacher. Take an exciting flight through the universe as spectacular stellar wonders fill a state-of -the-art domed theater. Call for show times (reservations recommended). (603) 271-STAR.

DANIEL WEBSTER BIRTHPLACE HISTORIC SITE (Grid L23:38) One of the United States' most distinguished statesmen and orators was born in this two-room frame house in 1782. Living history interpreters in period dress recreate the life of the times. Exhibits include Webster memorabilia. (603) 934-5057, (603) 547-3373.

FRANKLIN PIERCE HOMESTEAD HISTORIC SITE (Grid K26:44) This 1804 mansion offers a window to our past, and the childhood world of our 14th President, Franklin Pierce. (603) 478-3165.

FRANCONIA NOTCH STATE PARK (Grid L19:29) The park comprises 6,440 acres located in a deep valley between the Franconia and Kinsman mountain ranges. The New England Ski Museum, and Aerial Tramway to Cannon Mountain are located here. The park is also famous for such natural features as The Basin, a 20-foot glacial pothole, The Flume, a narrow, deep gorge, and The Old Man of the Mountain site, that was a natural granite profile 1200 feet above Profile Lake. (603) 823-8800.

LOST RIVER (Grid L19:29) Follow Lost River with the whole family as it appears and disappears through a narrow, steep walled gorge, tumbled granite, crevasses, caverns and falls. Lost River also features a geological display and nature garden with over 300 varieties of native flowers, ferns and shrubs. (603) 745-8031.

MOUNT MONADNOCK (Grid K26:44) One of the most frequently climbed mountains in the world offers 40 miles of trails and spectacular views from its 3,165-foot summit. (603) 532-8862.

MOUNT WASHINGTON COG RAILWAY (Grid N18:30) The world's first mountain-climbing cog railway opened in 1869. Take a three-hour round trip powered by a coal-fired steam engine up one of the steepest tracks in the world to the summit of the highest peak in the Northeast (6,288 ft). On a clear day there are spectacular views of the White Mountains, covering four states and Canada. Reservations are recommended. (603) 278-5404, (800) 922-8825.

ODIORNE POINT STATE PARK (Grid P26:39) Explore tide pools, salt marshes, World War II fortifications, or study marine life in the Seacoast Science Center. (603) 436-7406, (603) 436-8043.

ROBERT FROST FARM (Grid N26:45) The farm was the poet's home for ten years, from 1901-1909. Seasonal guided house tours are available. (603) 432-3091.

RUGGLES MINE (Grid K22:38) Explore for mica, feldspar, and beryl. First opened in 1803 at the top of Isinglass Mountain, "The mine in the sky" includes giant rooms and tunnels with arched ceilings that illustrate how the mountains were formed and eventually worn down. The site also has picnic tables with excellent Mount Cardigan views. (603) 523-4275.

Special Points of Interest

SAINT-GAUDENS NATIONAL HISTORIC SITE (Grid J22:37) One of America's most famous sculptors worked here among flower gardens and trees. Full-size castings and models are on display here, and concerts are held on the lawn. (603) 675-2175.

SQUAM LAKES NATURAL SCIENCE CENTER (Grid M21:29) This 200-acre nature center lets you observe black bear, river otters, bobcat and bald eagle in natural enclosures. There are gardens and a children's center with hands-on exhibits. In season, you can take a guided pontoon-boat cruise. (603) 968-7194.

STRAWBERY BANKE (Grid P25:39) With nine furnished houses from humble to aristocratic, authentic gardens and a 1943 grocery, Strawbery Banke is a 10-acre waterfront neighborhood and museum which spotlights one of the nation's first urban sites, illustrating 350 years of architectural and social change. (603) 433-1100.

WENTWORTH-COOLIDGE MANSION (Grid P25:39) A dominating 42-room structure that reflects three periods of New England architecture (1710-1750), the mansion was the official residence of Benning Wentworth, the first Royal Governor of New Hampshire (1741-1767). It contains the council chambers where the state's first provincial government conducted affairs. Lilacs on the grounds are descendants of the first brought into this country. (603) 436-6607.

RHODE ISLAND

BLITHEWOLD MANSION AND GARDENS (Grid N32:50) Blithewold is a 45-room bayside mansion with 33 acres of beautifully landscaped grounds and gardens featuring 50,000 varieties of flowering bulbs, as well as a 90-foot Giant Sequoia. (401) 253-2707.

BROWN UNIVERSITY (See Providence Insert - Page 76) Brown University held its first Commencement in 1769. The University was founded on principles of interdenominational cooperation, having as its original purpose the training of ministers. Brown's identity was forged in Rhode Island's rebellious, egalitarian and independent spirit. The University was named after Nicholas Brown Jr., one of New England's leading merchants who played a leading part in the economic and cultural life of the state. In addition to being the college's leading donor, Brown helped found Butler Hospital and the Providence Athenaeum. (401) 863-2378.

CASEY FARM (Grid M33:49) Operated by the Society For Preservation of New England Antiquities, this working farm is one of the original plantation farms of the Colonial era, complete with an 18th-Century house. You can take a tour and buy fresh produce. (401) 295-1030.

CLIFF WALK (Grid N33:50) Cliff Walk is 3.5 miles long, dramatically overlooking the Atlantic Ocean and many of Newport's famous mansions. (401) 849-4048.

GILBERT STUART BIRTHPLACE (Grid M33:49) Stuart was the foremost Colonial portraitist in America, best known for his portraits of George Washington. The house and grounds, including the recently restored grist mill, make this one of the more picturesque sites in the state. (401) 294-3001.

GREEN ANIMALS TOPIARY GARDEN (Grid N32:50) In 1880, Thomas E. Brayton began sculpting plants in the shape of animals and geometric figures on his estate overlooking Narragansett Bay. The house is filled with original Victorian furnishings and an antique toy collection. (401) 847-1000.

MCCOY STADIUM (See Providence Insert - Page 76) The recently renovated McCoy Stadium is an affordable, family-friendly place to see a ballgame. McCoy is home to the AAA minor-league affiliate of the Boston Red Sox. Many Sox stars, including Nomar Garciaparra, once played here. (401) 724-7300.

MUSEUM OF ART, RHODE ISLAND SCHOOL OF DESIGN (See Providence Insert - Page 76) The museum has a modest but inspiring collection of Old Masters, Egyptian and Etruscan artifacts, a nine-foot Japanese Buddha and Colonial-period Rhode Island furniture and silverware. (401) 454-6500.

RHODE ISLAND STATE CAPITOL (See Providence Insert) Built of majestic Georgia marble and modeled in part after St Peter's Basilica, the Capitol contains the original charter of 1663 granted by King Charles II, and Gilbert Stuart's full-length portrait of George Washington. (401) 277-2357.

ROGER WILLIAMS PARK (Grid N31:50) A wide variety of recreational activities are spread throughout the park's 422 acres. Exhibiting over 900 animals, the Roger Williams Park Zoo is nationally known. A recently opened exhibit, "The Marco Polo Trail", features camels, Asian black bears and snow leopards in a habitat that traces Marco Polo's explorations. The Museum of Natural History, Rhode Island's only Natural History Museum, includes the recently renovated Cormack Planetarium. Other attractions in the park include The Charles Smith Greenhouses, as well as Carousel Village, which offers a 60-rider carousel, pony rides, and a large playground. 1000 Elmwood Ave. (401) 785-3510.

SLATER MILL HISTORIC SITE (See Providence Insert - Page 76) Restored to its early 1800's appearance, the mill buildings depict factory production and life as it was lived in a 19th-Century industrial village. Guided tours are available from the 1758 Sylvanus Brown house, which offers demonstrations of hand spinning and weaving. Displays at Slater's Mill depict the transition from handcraft to machine production. The Wilkinson Mill built in 1810, makes use of a rebuilt 8-ton water wheel that is the only one of its kind in America. (401) 725-8638.

WATERPLACE PARK (See Providence Insert - Page 76) Connecting College Hill to a revitalized downtown, Waterplace Park is a beautifully landscaped riverside walk crossed by several Venetian-style bridges. You can even take a gondola ride. (401) 785-9450.

VERMONT

BEN & JERRY'S ICE CREAM FACTORY (Grid G18:28) Vermont's most popular tourist attraction features tours of the factory as well as free samples. (802) 882-1240.

BENNINGTON BATTLE MONUMENT (Grid F25:36) A 306-foot obelisk commemorates the Revolutionary War victory of John Stark and the Green Mountain Boys. Ride the elevator to the top for excellent views. (802) 447-0550.

BENNINGTON MUSEUM (Grid F26:42) The museum exhibits include works by Grandma Moses, military memorabilia, and centuries-old artifacts. (802) 447-1571.

CABOT CREAMERY (Grid J17:18) Enjoy a video and tour the factory. Watch dairy products being made and nibble your way around the gift shop. (800) 837-4261.

ETHAN ALLEN HOMESTEAD (Grid F17:17) Tour the home of Ethan Allen, Vermont's colorful Revolutionary War hero, including the restored 1787 farmhouse. The beautiful site along the Winooski River has hiking trails, and picnicking is allowed. (802) 865-4556.

EUREKA SCHOOLHOUSE (Grid H23:37) One of the few surviving 18th-Century public buildings in Vermont is furnished with a variety of educational materials. (802) 828-3051, (802) 885-3035.

HILDENE (Grid F24:36) Located on a promontory with marvelous views, walking trails and formal gardens, this 24-room mansion explores the life and times of Abraham Lincoln's oldest son, Robert Todd Lincoln, who summered here from 1905-1926. (802) 362-1788.

HUBBARDTON BATTLE MONUMENT (Grid F21:37) An interpretive exhibit on the only Revolutionary War battle fought in Vermont features an electronic map showing troop movements during the battle. (802) 759-2412, (802) 273-2282 (in season).

JUSTIN SMITH MORRILL HOMESTEAD (Grid J20:28) This furnished 17-room Gothic Revival cottage has several 19th-Century agricultural outbuildings. The icehouse and carriage barn have interpretive exhibits on the Land Grant College Acts authored by Morrill, Gothic Revival architecture, and period agricultural methods. (802) 828-3051, (802) 765-4484 (in season).

MONTSHIRE MUSEUM OF SCIENCE (Grid J21:28) Kids will enjoy the see-through beehive, laws-of-physics playground, and easy walking trails. (802) 649-2200.

MOUNT EQUINOX SKYLINE DRIVE (Grid F24:36) This drive features spectacular views of the Berkshires and White Mountains from the 3,835-foot peak of Mt. Equinox. At the summit, the Equinox Mountain Inn offers a fine dining experience. (802) 362-1115.

MOUNT INDEPENDENCE STATE HISTORIC SITE (Grid E21:37) A new Interpretive Center contains interactive exhibits and period artifacts. Seasonal living history encampments explore the life of a Revolutionary War soldier stationed atop Mount Independence, a bustling fort site in 1777. A boat stationed at Larabee's Point offers historic tours of Lake Champlain and Fort Ticonderoga. (802) 759-2412, (802) 948-2000 (in season).

OLD CONSTITUTION HOUSE (Grid J22:37) Vermont's Constitution was written here in 1777. An exhibit depicts the meaning of the document, and the events leading to statehood in 1795. (802) 672-3773.

PRESIDENT CALVIN COOLIDGE STATE HISTORIC SITE (Grid G22:37) Ten historic buildings are open in this historic village where Calvin Coolidge was born, raised, and sworn in as our 30th President in 1923. He is buried here with his wife Grace and seven generations of his family. (802) 672-3773.

PRESIDENT CHESTER ARTHUR BIRTHPLACE HISTORIC SITE (Grid G15:18) An interpretive exhibit in the Arthur house details the life and career of our 21st President. The brick church, where Arthur's father served as preacher, has also been restored. (802) 828-3051.

ROCK OF AGES QUARRIES (Grid H19:28) Peer 600 feet into one of the world's largest granite veins on a narrated bus tour of an active quarry The visitor's center offers video exhibits and fine gifts. (802) 476-3119.

SHELBURNE FARMS (Grid E17:17) Visit a working farm on an idyllic 1400-acre estate with landscaping by Frederick Law Olmsted and a five-story turreted barn. (802) 985-8686.

SHELBURNE MUSEUM (Grid E18:27) This museum is a fabulous collection of Americana. 80,000 objects are housed in 37 historic buildings include a schoolhouse, lighthouse, carousel, and steamboat. Tickets provide a two-day admission to the museum. (802) 985-3346.

SOUTHERN VERMONT ART CENTER (Grid F24:36) Ten galleries are housed in a National Historic Trust mansion. The Center also features sculpture gardens, a botany trail, hiking trails, and a cafe. (802) 362-1405.

STATE HOUSE (Grid H18:28) Built with local granite in the Doric style, the building's gold leaf dome supports a statue of Ceres, the goddess of agriculture. (802) 828-2228.

UNIVERSITY OF VERMONT (Grid F17:17) Vermont's largest institution of higher learning was founded in 1791. On campus, the Perkins Museum of Geology has exhibits on dinosaurs, fossils and rocks, as well as early granite quarrying in Vermont. The Robert Fleming museum has an impressive collection of 19,000 art objects from around the globe, spanning the history of civilization. (802) 656-3370.

VERMONT STATE CRAFT CENTER (Grid F20:27) Housed in an old mill building at Otter Creek Falls, the Center features the work of some of Vermont's finest artisans. (802) 388-3177.